Return to Glory

Return to Glory

Preaching Through Romans
(Romans 3:22–5:21)

Michael Eaton

paternoster
press

First Published in 1999 by Paternoster Press

05 04 03 02 01 00 99   7 6 5 4 3 2 1

Paternoster Press is an imprint of Paternoster Publishing,
PO Box 300, Carlisle, Cumbria, CA3 0QS, UK
http://www.paternoster-publishing.com

British Library Cataloguing in Publication Data
A catalogue record for this book is available from the British Library.

ISBN 0-85364-953-7

Cover Design by Mephisto, Glasgow
Typeset by WestKey Ltd, Falmouth, Cornwall
Printed in Great Britain by
Caledonian International Book Manufacturing Ltd, Glasgow

Contents

Preface

These expositions of Romans 3:22b–5:21 are abridged versions of 'messages' originally preached in Kenya and in India. Some of them were preached in City Hall, Nairobi, others in Nairobi Cinema, and other fellowships also heard parts of this material, or summaries of it: churches in the Busia district of western Kenya when I travelled there with a team of young friends, at the turn of the year 1992/1993; a 'kesha' (overnight fellowship meeting) in Kawangware, Nairobi, in January 1993; friends in the training centre of the New Frontiers churches in Goa, India, in October 1993. All of these friends were receptive and stimulating congregations and I grew in my understanding of Romans as we thought about it together and as I did my best to answer questions. The chapters on Romans 4 were drafted in the home of my friends Abiud and Mary Kimathi while I was staying there and preaching on Romans in Kisumu, on the edge of Lake Victoria, in July 1994.

Numerous articles and works on Paul have helped me, and I have about two dozen commentaries on Romans within reach, plus the resources of my own library of several thousand books, others consulted in libraries, and my own previous expositions which I have reconsidered along the way. C.T. Rhyne's book *Faith Establishes the Law* (Scholars

Press 1981) led me to see 3:31 as looking forwards as well as backwards. There are similar debts too many to mention. Recently, in 1997, I have been preaching through these chapters yet again in southern India.

There is a tendency among New Testament scholars to reinterpret Paul's teaching concerning 'justification'. The classic evangelical teaching which goes back to the Protestant Reformation, back to Paul himself, and further still back to Genesis 15:6 has been largely discarded. Yet the classic teaching concerning justification is a vital foundation in the church, and the modern ways of returning to old Pharisaism and catholicism will bring no blessing to anyone directly. If we have teaching about sanctification but no teaching about justification, our sanctification itself will be twisted. Justification by faith is central and basic in the gospel. If we lose sight of it now, our evangelicalism will die, our charismatic movement will die, our revival will die, but the kingdom of God will continue and preachers of the gospel will find a new name for themselves!

The idea in some circles is that first-century Judaism was not legalistic in the way that Paul describes it in Romans. Jews thought they were saved by God's entering into covenant with them (so the idea goes). The law is not a way of 'getting in' to God's people. It is only a way of 'staying in'.

However, such an approach is still legalism. Paul attacked 'staying in' by law as much as if not more than he attacked 'getting in' by law. When Paul asked 'Are you now being made perfect by the flesh?' it was 'staying in' by keeping the law that he had in mind. I am afraid 'covenantal nomism', as it is called, is itself legalistic, and the scholars who want to defend it are themselves closer to the men of Acts 15:1 than they are to Paul.

'The New Perspective on Paul' is often stimulating, and is right in affirming that the cultural aspect of Paul's teaching needs considering, but I still think the Reformation approach to Paul is fruitful and basically correct. My comments in Chapter 15 will reveal that I reject the idea that Paul's doctrine of justification needs to be amended to find a way to bring the law back in! Neither 'coming in' or 'staying in' the kingdom of God is by the Mosaic covenant or by 'works'.

Although scholarly writings are my daily food, there is no scholarly apparatus in this book. It tries to be free from distractions. All translations from the Bible are my own. On the other hand I know well the various revisions of the Authorized Version. If my translations resemble that tradition I shall not be surprised.

My family have encouraged my many years of Romans study. A long time ago, when I first preached through Romans over the course of four years, my wife Jenny scribbled notes of what I was preaching. Her notes were often fuller than my own, and I have frequently consulted them. My son, Calvin Eaton, has given his time and his expertise with computers to this project, and has rescued me from various word-processing crises. What would I do without him? My daughter Tina Gysling has given me some good editorial advice and I am grateful.

I am again grateful to Mrs Florence Okumu who read earlier versions of this project. Other friends who make suggestions, and generally keep me motivated and encouraged as I preach through Romans, are much appreciated. This work is the better for their recommendations as I write and preach. They are precious to me indeed.

What was new to me when I preached through these chapters again was the conviction I came to that our being 'in Adam' by way of representation is based upon Adam's being one with us in life but this order is reversed in Jesus (see Chapters 53 and 55). Jesus comes to represent us and then we come to be 'in Christ'. This would solve a number of problems theologians have had with the nature of our union with Adam. It is a possibility that was not considered in G.P. Hutchinson's *The Problem of Original Sin in American Presbyterian Theology* (Presbyterian and Reformed 1972), one of the fullest books on this particular point.

As always, it is the Chrisco people of Nairobi for whom this material was preached and written. For the blessing of having them as my 'laboratory' where this material is first shared I am ever grateful.

Michael Eaton,
Nairobi, August 1997

1

There is no Difference (Romans 3:22b–23)

In Romans 3:21–22a Paul puts forward a basic statement of the gospel. It contains eight basic principles, which I can list as follows.

1. Jesus starts a new epoch in the history of the world.
2. Salvation is a matter of being clothed or covered by a righteousness that is not ours.
3. This righteousness comes entirely from God.
4. This righteousness comes without the law.
5. The law and all the other Scriptures witness and prophesy what God would do through Jesus.
6. Salvation comes to us through the faithfulness of Jesus Christ.
7. Salvation is received by faith.
8. Salvation is designed for everyone in the human race.

What Paul does from this point is develop and expand what he has said in 3:21–22a.

First of all he develops the point that salvation in Jesus is available for everyone. He has said, 'But now . . . a righteousness from God has been manifested . . . to *all* who believe'. Now he develops this word 'all'. The reason why this salvation is for everyone is because everyone needs it. There are no fundamental differences between the various types of people in the human race. The gospel is for all who believe, *for there is no difference* (Rom.3:22b).

Of course there are differences among men and women in many ways. But in the things that really matter Paul says 'there is no difference'. He is not saying there are no differences at all. He is saying there is no difference in the availability of the gospel. It is needed by everyone, *for all have sinned and lack the glory of God* (Rom.3:23).

There is no difference with regard to wealth.

It is true that the gospel is tailor-made for the poor (James 2:5), but the poor and the rich both need the gospel. The capitalist may think socialists are needy and wicked. The socialist may think capitalists are needy and wicked. Various political parties think the others are somehow morally deficient. The truth is, in the matter of needing a saviour 'there is no difference'.

Once I was watching a political broadcast in a foreign country. Two heads of two political parties were debating with each other on national television. One party leader accused the other party leader of this crime and that broken promise. Then the second one accused the first of violence and hidden corruption. But for anyone who knew the life of the country, both were right! When two sinners accuse each other normally both of them are right. When the rich and the poor accuse each other both are right. Employers and employees are normally equally correct when they press their claims against each other. When political parties point out each other's sins they are normally both perceptive, observant and entirely right! There is no difference . . . All have sinned.

There is no difference in nationalities or tribes.

Often one country will accuse another country, or one tribe will accuse another tribe. The north of the country accuses the south of the country and vice versa. So do the east and the west, the northern hemisphere and the southern hemisphere, the black and the white and so on. But there is no difference in this particular matter. All have sinned.

There is no difference between male and female.

'Feminists' may point to the poor record of men; they are normally right. But if any feminist friend wants to tell me men are worse than they are I can at least express my doubts! All have sinned! Men sin; women sin. There is no difference!

There is no difference in educated and uneducated.

One tends to think of uneducated people as somehow more degraded and wicked. Are they any worse than the intellectuals? Not at all. How wicked some famous 'intellectuals' have been! There are ignorant sinners and clever sinners, but in the matter of needing Jesus Christ 'there is no difference'.

There is no difference between temperaments.

The Greeks divided types of human personality into four groups. It is certainly observable that there are different types of personality and the Greek fourfold classification is helpful, although people have tendencies that are characteristic of more than one category.

The 'phlegmatic' sinners are seemingly flat and unemotional and pride themselves on their calmness but are full of pride and quiet bitterness. They sit back and express shock that anyone could do such things as other sinners do. The 'choleric' sinners lose their temper and can be wicked in their wild rages, their carelessness in relationships, their poor team spirit. The 'melancholic' temperament produces people who are wicked in their unbelief and cynicism. The 'sanguine' sinners are outgoing and relaxed and yet are thoughtless and inconsiderate.

Yes, we sin in different ways and have different temptations. But no one is in a position to be self-righteous. All have sinned! Why do we feel that we are different? One reason is the strange blindness that comes over us when we are considering ourselves. We are capable of criticizing others but sensitive and touchy when we are criticized ourselves. But we all need a Saviour! We are all capable of seeing the speck in the other person's eye but not so aware of the plank of wood in our own. We are all hypocrites by nature. We pretend to be better than others and we talk about others with a superior tone. But there is no difference; all have sinned.

Later on in this letter to the Romans (10:12), Paul will say once again 'There is no difference'. It is also true that there is no difference because 'The same Lord . . . richly blesses all who call on him'. We are one in sin and there is one Saviour for all of us. 'There is no difference' between us in sin, but 'There is no difference' between us in the way of salvation.

2

All Have Sinned (Romans 3:23)

God's salvation is for everyone because everyone needs it. There is no difference, Paul says, *For all have sinned and lack the glory of God* (Rom.3:23).

It is a fact that everyone has sinned.

The Bible is constantly asserting it. 'There is not a person who does not sin' (1 Kgs. 8:46). 'If you hold in mind a person's sins, O Lord, who could stand?' (Ps. 130:3). 'There is not a living person who is righteous before you' (Ps. 143:2). 'All have sinned' does not refer to our sinning 'in Adam'. The tense does not have to mean 'something done once and for ever', as some think. The Greek tense (which scholars call an 'aorist') may have the force of summarizing something which has been true for a long time. The right translation is 'All have sinned'. It is not that 'All sinned' in Adam. That only gets mentioned in Romans 5. Our own actual sins in our own lifetime are being mentioned here. Paul's point is that no person on earth has ever been free from sin except Jesus. People do not like the word 'sin', yet it does not take great perceptiveness to see deceit and pride and hypocrisy and prejudice and lovelessness on all sides – and in our own hearts!

Sin is failing to be and to do what God wants.

It is opposition to God, not wanting his way in our lives. It is corrupt thoughts, corrupt plans, corrupt deeds, corrupt desires. It is pride, lifting ourselves up in our own estimate. It is selfishness. In relation to God it is rebellion. In relation to others it is lovelessness. In relation to ourselves it is self-centredness.

Sin is instinctively denied.

Paul has been spending almost three chapters of Romans insisting on human sin. Why is he spending so much time on the subject? Because it is a subject we avoid. Yet salvation is salvation from sin, before it is anything else. We have to see the seriousness of sin if we are to see the greatness of salvation. Some deny sin altogether. They explain it away. We are determined by our chemistry, they say, and so we do not really have any freedom. There is no such thing as sin – so they say. Or they say it is imaginary, or just a matter of unpleasant feelings when we go against certain social taboos.

Others admit there is such a thing as sin but they deny that *they* have sinned. We find reasons why what we are and what we do is not really blameworthy. We are 'as good as anyone else'. We justify sin.

But the truth is: all have sinned. We have truly and really and accountably done things and thought things and said things and planned things that are wicked. Sin is selfishness

– and we have all been guilty. Sin is godlessness – and we have all acted in rebellion against the God of the Bible. Sin is missing what God wants in our lives and we have all acted in such a way.

Underlying the fact about our actions is a fact about our nature.

He states a fact ('For all have sinned . . . ') and then points to an underlying deficiency (' . . . and lack the glory of God'). 'All have sinned' refers to what we have done. 'And lack the glory of God' tells us something about the way we are by nature, the way we came into this world. Glory is the outshining of holiness. When humankind was created by God it was invested with 'glory'. Men and women were made in the image of God. We were Godlike in character. Then something went wrong. The story in Genesis 3 is the story of a fall in the human race. Before that event, humankind was carrying the mark of God's holy and righteous character. In some way it was even visible. Men and women were made to walk around on planet earth with a visible righteousness. They were created with a capacity for personal relationships and good fellowship. They were in a position where they could enjoy a sweet harmonious relationship to God. They were able to have dominion in a creative way over God's world like a shepherd, tending and caring for God's world and bringing the best out of it. This is the glory of God that men and women were intended to have, and that redeemed and restored men and women will have again. But in our present state, all have sinned and we lack the glory of God. This shows us what a terrible disaster sin is. It is to be deprived of that radiating righteousness that God originally gave.

In Jesus this 'glory of God' comes back to us, but that is not Paul's point here. His point here is that the entire human race have sinned in actual fact and are badly in need of the 'righteousness of God' that Paul is writing about. Worse still their state is one of deprivation. They have come into this world with a deficiency. They lack the glory of God that was originally intended.

How ugly is sin. Our very nature has been distorted and twisted by our sinfulness. We have twisted motivations. Nothing we ever do is as good as it should be. Nothing in us is capable of earning God's goodness towards us. By nature every person is unresponsive towards God.

No doubt some sins are worse than others. But all have enough sin to make eternal separation from God an act of justice. All have enough sin to close the doors of heaven against them – without a Saviour. All have enough sin to pollute their lives and their relationships – unless they find Jesus to rescue them.

Paul puts this bad news before us, but happily he moves on to good news speedily. 'They are justified, as a gift, by his grace, through the redemption that is in Christ Jesus'. A free salvation is what we need.

3

A Righteousness not my Own
(Romans 3:24)

Romans 3:21–31 is a very compressed piece of writing. We must try to keep the whole in our minds and yet we also want to take a close look at each individual part. Verses 21–22a began by putting before us, who are now among Paul's readers, eight basic truths of the Christian message. Paul is now developing these themes. He has expanded the point about everyone needing salvation (3:22b–23).

Now he expands the point that salvation is a matter of being clothed or covered by a righteousness that is not ours. Everyone has sinned. There is only one way of being 'righteous' before God. It has to be a matter of a *gift* of righteousness. Now he goes on: *They are justified, as a gift, by his grace through the redemption that is in Christ Jesus* (Rom. 3:24).

What does it mean to be 'justified'? It means to be covered with a righteousness that is not one's own but which belongs to Jesus. Our condemnation as sinners is reversed by a pronouncement that we are righteous.

The importance of 'being justified by his grace'.

There are churches that are muddled when it comes to justification by faith. I have friends that are energetic Christians who are nevertheless quite confused about the matter. They love Jesus. They are full of the power of the Spirit. Yet they have weaknesses because they do not see that they are justified exclusively by the blood and righteousness of Christ and not at all by how well they are doing in their obedience to the Lord Jesus. However their weaknesses do not destroy them. On the other side there are churches which seem only to know the doctrine of justification that are harsh and cold. God certainly does not seem to be blessing them. They are not much of a blessing to others and their influence upon unsaved people is microscopic.

The reality of regeneration and continual life by the Holy Spirit is the characteristic of a living church! A person who knows about new birth but knows little about justification may be blessed indeed. But a person who knows a lot about justification but little about new birth and the power of the Holy Spirit is in bad trouble! Some great saints have been people of spiritual power before they become clear about justification by faith.

However justification is vitally important and the church of Jesus is weakened if Christians do not realize clearly that they stand before God only by Christ's righteousness and not at all by their own righteousness. I would not say justification is the 'heart' of the gospel to the extent that anyone who is muddled about it is not a Christian. I would rather say it is the 'foundation' of the gospel. It underlies the gospel.

Without a clear understanding of justification of faith there cannot be much assurance. If we do not see that we stand before God only by the righteousness of Christ, our holiness becomes a rather legalistic matter. Without an understanding of justification by faith the gospel tends to be heavy news rather than good news! Without a recognition of justification by God's grace we tend to be Pharisaical in our relationships with others.

The imagery, the picture-language, of the doctrine.

Talk about justification is using the picture-language of a lawcourt. There are different ways of picturing God. He may be pictured as a father, a shepherd, a king, a farmer, a husband. When we talk about justification, we are using the language of a lawcourt. God is being pictured as a judge and king. In the ancient world a king was also a judge.

Consider what the teaching presupposes.

The idea of being justified makes a number of assumptions. It assumes that our sin is real. God's wrath is against all sin. Justification assumes that in ourselves God the righteous judge must condemn us and take action against us. It takes for granted that God is righteous and holy. It also assumes that any kind of righteousness by good deeds of our own is impossible. Even Jewish people seeking righteousness by law-keeping find their way is blocked. Justification takes it for granted that the obedience and the sin-bearing of Jesus on the cross can be applied to us so as to totally change our relationship to God.

'Being justified by his grace' also assumes that this situation continues after we have been saved. It is not that we are saved and become righteous and thereafter are accepted because we are righteous in Jesus. Our acceptance with God is always because of the righteousness of Jesus. It is taken that we are never righteous enough to stand before God in our own righteousness. It is always true that self-justification is impossible. We shall never be able to stand before God in any other way. But through Jesus we can stand before God righteous in his sight, right now! Notice Paul says we *are* 'justified', covered with Christ's righteousness, now! It is not 'and we shall be justified . . . '. No, it starts now! Now, as soon as we believe in Jesus Christ, we are the other side of judgment day! We have been through judgment day. God has already pronounced us 'not guilty'. Though in ourselves we were guilty, God pronounces us 'not guilty'. We are released from condemnation and guilt. We are innocent, pure, clean, righteous in God's eyes as if we had been as obedient as Jesus. Justification never alters in a child of God. When we believe in Jesus, immediately the righteousness of Jesus is reckoned as being ours. It is instantaneous. It takes place instantly in the courts of heaven. I do not have to fear judgment day, because (with reference to my

eternal salvation) it is a past event. I have gone through it.
The issue is closed. The judge of all the universe tells me I
am acquitted. I can go free.

4

Justified by his Grace (Romans 3:24)

Let us take a closer look at what it means to be 'justified'.

It is not something that takes place inside our hearts. It is something that takes place outside of us, in the heart of God. It is a decision taken about us, not a work done in us. This is why it does not matter at this point how we feel or how obedient we are. Our righteousness does not help justification. Our sinfulness does not hinder justification. Justification is when the righteousness of Jesus is credited to us. It is a righteousness that comes from outside of us altogether.

The word 'justify' means 'to declare righteous'. There are four ways of showing this. Firstly, to 'justify' is the opposite of to 'condemn'. Romans 8:33,34 says, 'It is God who justifies. Who shall condemn?' Justification is the opposite of condemnation. What does condemnation mean? Does it mean 'make sinful'? No, when you condemn someone, you are not making them wicked, you are declaring them wicked in some way or other. Justification is not making someone righteous; it is declaring that person righteous. It is true that in the new birth God makes us a new person and gives us the Spirit. But even before he gives us the Spirit and changes our nature he declares that we are righteous with someone else's righteousness. We are declared righteous with the righteousness of Jesus Christ. This is justification. Keep justification and new birth distinct in your thinking!

Another way of showing the same point is to consider the phrase 'justifying God'. In Luke 7:29 we read that the people 'justified God' (a literal translation). Does this mean that they made God righteous? No, it means that they acknowledged or declared that God is righteous. Justification is a declaration!

The same thing becomes clear when we consider the phrase 'justifying oneself'. In Luke 10:29 we read of a man who asked Jesus a question about the greatest commandment. Jesus said, 'Love the Lord . . . and love your neighbour'. Then we read 'But wanting to justify himself, he asked Jesus, "And who is my neighbour?".' Consider the phrase 'wanting to justify himself'. Does it mean that he was wrong but wanted to make himself right? No! It means he was wanting to present himself as a righteous person. He was wanting to declare himself righteous.

Then another way of showing that the word 'justify' does not mean 'to make righteous' but 'to declare righteous' is to consider the equivalent expressions that are used. To be justified is to be 'reckoned' righteous (Rom. 4:4,5,6,8,9,10, 11,23). When you reckon someone as righteous, you do not make them righteous but you treat them that way, you count upon them being that way. It is not something you make them be; it is something you declare them to be. This is all vitally important. You will never have any deep and solid assurance and joy unless you get hold of this.

I live in Africa. I like to say justification is living on a 'borrowed' righteousness. Of course we in Africa have a different approach to borrowing to Westerners. Sometimes Western countries give a financial loan to a developing country in Africa. But in Africa we do not normally repay debts in the way Westerners expect. In the matter of international loans, for example, we tend to borrow but not give back! After all – we argue – Westerners are richer than we are. Westerners lent it to us because they had it spare. But we still need it and the people of the West are not in so much need. Westerners have plenty and don't need hard currency as much as we do, so why should we give it back? We tend to say to the West, 'When you gave it to us it was because you could afford it and we were in need. But you can still afford it and we are still in need! So why should you ask for it back?!'

So I can say we are 'borrowing' the righteousness of Jesus as clothing with which to stand before God. But since we are always going to need it we have no plans to give it back! We are permanently living on someone else's righteousness!

Let us take a closer look at the the generosity of God's justification.

Paul uses two expressions. Romans 3:24 says: 'They are justified as a gift, by his grace, through the redemption that is in Christ Jesus.'

We are justified 'freely' or 'as a gift'. This word comes in John 15:25, where it is said that Jesus was hated 'without a cause'. There was no reason why Jesus should have been hated. His enemies hated him 'freely, as a gift!'. There was no cause in Jesus why he should have been hated. A similar word comes in Acts 8:20 where Peter protests, 'May your silver go to perdition with you! Because you thought to get *the gift* of God through money!' Something similar could be said about justification. 'May your righteousness go to perdition, if you think you can get *the gift* of righteousness through any goodness of your own!'

We are justified 'by his grace'. Grace is God's totally undeserved kindness, his spontaneous love. It is the opposite of deserving something. It is the opposite of having worked for something.

It is 'daring' to believe this. You and I are being asked to believe that by faith in Jesus we are so clothed with the righteousness of Jesus that it is as if we were Jesus himself. No matter what I may be in myself I stand before God as righteous as Jesus is righteous. I am living on the righteousness of Jesus. This clothing will never wear out. I have been given it for ever. Is this gospel really as wonderful as this? Yes it is. We stand before God only by the righteousness of Jesus. Trust in Jesus and his righteousness is yours.

5

Redemption (Romans 3:24)

We are justified 'as a gift, by his grace, through the redemption that is in Christ Jesus'.

Paul is clarifying his message about salvation. He has said that salvation is a matter of being clothed or covered by a righteousness that is not ours. It is entirely free, entirely a gift of God's grace.

Now Paul says more. This gift of covering righteousness is 'through the redemption that is in Christ Jesus'. He is referring to the death of Jesus upon the cross, and to what Jesus did by means of his death. Paul has a particular word that he uses to describe what Jesus did on the cross: it is the word 'redemption'. 'Redemption' means 'the release of a slave by the paying of a price'. It was used literally in the ancient world of the payment that was needed to release a slave from his slavery. It was also used in Old Testament times of the payment that was needed to release an animal which should be slaughtered. The first-born animals were liable to be killed in sacrifice, but could be 'redeemed'. Payment could be made for their release from death. It was also used of the payment made for a person in situations when he was liable to the death penalty. For example, a person whose animal had killed someone was himself liable to be executed, but he could be released from condemnation by the payment of a price.

This is the kind of picture-language being used here. We may be 'justified' – released from condemnation and death penalty and declared righteous – through the price-paying of Jesus upon the cross.

There are four things, at least, involved in Paul's using this word to speak of Jesus' death upon the cross for us.

It implies that we were in some kind of slavery.

The slavery was slavery to guilt and condemnation. We were slaves to the committing of sin. We could not stop sinning. We were slaves to the guilt of sin. Sin condemned and we could not release ourselves from its condemnation. We were under the wrath of God and could do nothing to extricate ourselves from our plight.

It implies that there is a way of release from the slavery we were in.

We were in bondage to condemnation and death-penalty, but the dying of Jesus released us by the payment of a price so that we could be 'justified', fully righteous in the eyes of God. The death of Jesus was a mighty act of release from condemnation. We were redeemed from the curse of the law.

It implies that our release from slavery was costly.

Jesus 'ransomed' us. He paid a price that released us from our slavery, and that price was his death upon the cross. He gave his life as a 'ransom for many' (Matt. 20:28). He 'gave himself to redeem us from all iniquity' (Tit. 2:14). The price he paid was 'the precious blood, like that of a lamb without blot on it and without any blemish, that is the blood of Christ' (1 Pet. 2:28). We have 'redemption through his blood' (Eph. 1:7). It is not necessary to ask the question: 'Who was the price paid to?' The word is only a picture-word, an illustration. It does not have to be pressed. The point is not that the blood of Jesus had to be paid 'to' someone. The point is simply that our release from guilt and death penalty was exceedingly costly to the Father, and costly to Jesus himself. The cost of such a redemption was that Christ was made a curse for us (Gal. 3:13).

It implies that we are now free.

The word in Romans 3:24 means something like 'redemption-away'. We are justified through the payment that takes us away altogether from condemnation. It means that we are taken out of condemnation, and also that we are brought into sonship and freedom. We were 'bought' by the blood of Christ (see 1 Cor. 6:18–20). God 'bought the church' (Acts 20:28).

How does justification, being declared righteous, come through the cross? He ransomed us from condemnation by taking the condemnation upon himself. He was our substitute. The wrath of God fell on Jesus instead of falling on us. By his being willing to pay such a price Jesus 'ransomed us away' from condemnation.

The human race was in the prison of guilt. We ought to be abandoned by God altogether. But suddenly we hear that a substitution has taken place. The man Jesus has stepped into our place. It is as though he has sinned all of the sins of the entire human race. Our condemnation is transferred to him. He suffers the curse of God, 'the curse of the law' (Gal. 3:13). The ancient law of Deuteronomy had explained that anyone who was executed by hanging on a tree was under the curse of God. Jesus dies in precisely that way, 'under the curse of the law'. Because he is executed instead of us, we can go free. Not only are our sins transferred to him, his obedience is transferred to us. The entire human race is 'in Christ' as he dies for the human race upon the cross. It is an act of ransoming the human race. It is for everyone. 'All have sinned . . . being justified by his grace . . . through the redemption that is in Christ Jesus.' It is not that everyone will eventually go to heaven: some people will be eternally lost. Yet (as in 2 Cor. 5) Paul says that everyone in the entire human race has been redeemed and each person has 'died' to what he or she was.

The way in which Scripture presents this matter is to say that our salvation has been accomplished. We have been saved! But this salvation has to be endorsed, ratified, seconded. In some types of democratic meeting, if a motion

is put before the meeting, nothing happens unless it is
'seconded'. So it is with our salvation. It has been done! It
is ready and available! The message is: 'come for all things
are ready'.

6

Propitiation (Romans 3:25a)

Paul is expanding the point that salvation is a matter of being covered by a righteousness that is not ours. Every-one has sinned. The only way of salvation is to be given God's gift of righteousness. It comes to us freely as a gift, and it comes 'through the redemption that is in Christ Jesus'. Paul is continuing to clarify what was happening when Jesus died for us. He goes on: *God put him forward as a sacrifice to turn away anger, through faith and by means of blood* (Rom. 3:25a).

Here we come to the heart of the gospel. This is the most marvellous verse in the entire epistle to the Romans. The Lord Jesus Christ died upon the cross as a sacrifice that turns away the wrath of God. Let us look at it one word at a time.

'God put him forward'. The Greek word here can mean 'destined' or 'put forward'. I think 'put forward' is the best translation. The passage is dealing with what God did on the cross, not what he did in his eternal plan. It is like Galatians 3:1 which says God 'placarded' or 'publicly por-trayed' Jesus on the cross. God held up Jesus for all of the world to see. This is God's way of salvation. He has 'put forward' Jesus as the answer to the world's need.

'God put him forward as a sacrifice to turn away anger'. The Greek word used to be translated 'propitiation' (as in the Authorized Version of 1611). That is an excellent translation except that few people know the meaning of 'propitiation' nowadays! It is an old word which means 'a sacrifice which turns away anger'. The idea is that God was angry towards sin. He was determined to punish sin. But he put forward Jesus. Jesus carried our sins in his own body on the cross. It was as though Jesus were the sinner. God allowed the judgment for sin to come upon Jesus instead of coming upon us. So God's anger against our sin was turned away because it fell on Jesus instead of falling upon us.

'God put him forward as a sacrifice to turn away anger, *through faith*.' God's wrath against our sin will not actually be turned away until we believe. It is there for us, but it will not be experienced unless we put our faith in Jesus Christ.

'God put him forward as a sacrifice to turn away anger, through faith, and *by means of blood*.' The Greek wording is not one phrase, 'through-faith-in-his-blood', but two phrases, 'through faith (and) by his blood'. The phrase emphasizes that the sacrifice that turned away God's wrath from us was a sacrifice-of-blood. In the Old Testament God taught Israel in many different ways that sin gets remedied in the sight of God by the execution of a substitute. When Israel was redeemed from the land of Egypt the event that released them was the shedding of the blood of a lamb. In the tabernacle and later in the temple animals were sacrificed daily to make the same point. No blood, no atoning sacrifice. No atoning sacrifice, no forgiveness!

This is what was needed for us to be justified, declared righteous before God. The blood of the Son of God had to

be shed. It had to be given to God. It has to be received by
the people.

The cross is a great mystery.

The reasons why Christians believe in the teaching about
the cross of Jesus Christ is that we believe that God has
revealed to us that this is the way it is.

The cross tells us of the great evil of sin.

Sin is exceedingly offensive to God. It arouses his righteous
indignation and his determination to punish it and remove
it from his universe.

The cross tells us that Jesus is our substitute.

God transferred his antagonism towards sin to his Son and
allowed his wrath against sin to fall on him instead of upon
us. He died 'on our behalf' (Rom. 5:8).

The cross tells us that the wrath of God has been removed from us once we have put our faith in Jesus.

We need never fear that God is angry with us. God never
needs to punish us for our sins. The punishment was
consumed and swallowed up by Jesus' death on the cross.

When I see the cross by faith I can have assurance that I am justified.

This is Paul's point. We are 'justified through the redemp-tion that is in Christ Jesus. God put him forward as a sacrifice to turn away anger. . . .' When I have Jesus, the blood of Jesus turns God's anger away from me. In some mysterious way God is willing to accept the death of Jesus as something that clears my guilt away. God provided Jesus as my substitute. God laid on him the iniquity of us all. By his stripes I am healed. He died the righteous one in the place of the unrighteous ones.

Without the blood of Jesus everyone is in danger. God hates sin. Sin inevitably gets punished.

Under the blood of Jesus there is safety. God's anger has been turned away. I need never fear God's anger is against me. True, he can be angry in the sense of being a vexed Father. But he cannot be angry with me in the sense of threatening me with hell.

This propitiation, this sacrifice that turns away God's wrath, comes from God himself. It is not that the Father was angry and Jesus lovingly blocked the anger of the Father. Not at all! God − God the Father − so loved the world that he gave his Son. It was his idea. The love of God for me sent someone to turn away his own anger against my sin.

There is safety in the blood of Jesus, safety against God's judgment of sin. It is the blood of God's Son that allows him to say to me, 'I pronounce you righteous in my sight'.

7

Just and Justifier (Romans 3:25b–26)

It is the death of Jesus upon the cross as sin-bearer and substitute that enables God to 'justify' anyone who has Jesus as Saviour.

He did this to show his righteousness, because of his passing over the sins previously committed, in his divine forbearance of God (Rom. 3:25–26a). *It was for the purpose of showing his right-eousness in the present time, so that he might be just and the justifier of the person who has the faithfulness of Jesus* (Rom. 3:26b). God sent Jesus to the cross to pay the price of sin, to bear God's anger against sin.

In the cross God was making a declaration.

'He did this to show his righteousness. . . .' 'Righteous-ness' must refer to the character of God, as the rest of the argument will show. The cross demonstrates God's justice. Sin is a foul ugly blot on the universe. Is God unjust? Will sin go unpunished? And if God forgives sin is God being unjust and allowing sin to go unpunished? None of this is true. Sin is punished! Even in the case of those who are forgiven, sin is punished. Jesus died and accepted the punishment of sin in his own person on the cross. It is a

public declaration. God is utterly just and fair and righteous. Sin never goes unpunished. However the punishment can be transferred, and it was transferred from us to
God's Son.

One special reason why God wished to declare his
righteousness was because of the days before Jesus came.
'He did this to show his righteousness, because of his passing
over the sins previously committed'. The time before the
coming of Jesus was a time when many sins were committed. Yet God did not bring in the final judgment and end
of the world. Many people had fellowship with him and
their sins were 'passed over'. The word Paul chooses is a
word that almost means forgive, yet it is not quite the word
forgive. What is Paul's point? It is that the sins of believers
were 'passed over'. They were forgiven in a fashion and yet
the price of their forgiveness had not yet been paid. Old
Testament believers were forgiven on account of what was
about to happen but it had not happened yet. Before the
cross God could have been accused of not bothering about
sin. He could have been accused of favouring sin. He allows
it and does nothing about it, and 'passes over' the sins of
his people. It all seems so unjust.

Not any more! True, he had passed over sins 'in his
divine forbearance' (Rom. 3:26a). But after many centuries
God sends his Son to the cross. 'It was for the purpose of
showing his righteousness in the present time, so that he
might be just and the justifier of the person who has the
faithfulness of Jesus.'

In the cross God vindicates his character.

He shows how intensely pure he is, how much he hates sin. How serious his wrath will be in judgment day for those who are not under the shelter of the blood of Jesus. Everything that fell on Jesus will fall upon those who do not have Jesus, in that day of reckoning.

This means too that all sins – backwards and forwards in time – were dealt with upon the cross. Abraham and David and all of the great godly men and women of the Old Testament days were forgiven and justified by virtue of what God would do. Their sins were all passed over. But then Jesus comes and he atones for the sins of the entire human race, backwards and forwards in time.

In the cross there is both mercy and justice. There is mercy and love there for God is commending his love and showing a way of forgiveness and reconciliation to him. But that is only half of the truth. There is justice in the cross as well. God is 'just and the justifier of the person who has the faithfulness of Jesus'.

God is 'just and justifier' at the same time. It is an amazing combination. He is able to righteously condemn and punish sin and yet at the same time tell each one of his people, 'I pronounce that you are righteous.' It is the cross that makes justification possible.

To come to salvation we need to have 'the faithfulness of Jesus'. One should not translate this 'faith in Jesus'. The phrase here is identical to the phrase in Romans 4:16 which speaks of 'the one who is of the faith of Abraham'. No one would translate it 'faith in Abraham' in 4:16. Why should

anyone translate it 'faith in Jesus' in 3:26? The expressions
are the same. The point is that Jesus had perfect faith and
faithfulness. Our faith is not faith in our faith! It is simply
holding to Jesus' faith, or to Jesus' faithfulness.

This is the gospel! We are justified by our having the
obedience and righteousness of Jesus reckoned as ours.
When Jesus is mine everything he did for me comes to me.
His cross banishes my guilt. The punishment for my sins
that was hanging over me is swallowed up by the blood of
Jesus. He gives me his righteousness and he gives me
everything else as well that I need. Only obedience can
make God say to anyone 'You are righteous'. But I was
never able to produce a perfect obedience. Jesus has pro-
duced a perfect obedience for me. I never was capable of
paying the price for my sins, but Jesus has paid the price of
my sins for me. So when I have Jesus my sins are gone,
punished in him and never to be attributed to me. His
righteousness is mine. This justification is irreversible. God
will not reverse it. The devil cannot reverse it. My faith
shall never fail for Jesus intercedes for me at the right hand
of the Father. It is God who justifies! Who is the one that
shall condemn? No one!

8

Boasting Excluded (Romans 3:27)

At the point we have reached in Paul's great letter, he has presented a basic statement of the gospel (3:21–22a) and has then explained further (3:22b–26, beginning with 'For . . .' in verse 22b). Now he asks a question ('Where then is the boasting?') and he goes on to show three things that follow from this gospel that he has described.

The first consequence of all that he has said is: that the gospel totally excludes any form of boasting in one's achievement. *Where is the boasting then? It is excluded. By what law? By the law of works? No, by the law of faith* (Rom. 3:27).

This question comes to us as a test of whether we really see the gospel for what it is. Paul adds verses 27–31 because the three things he says in verses 27–28, verses 29–30 and in verse 31 each clarify the gospel.

One of the greatest tests of our experience of salvation is what we are boasting in.

If salvation is by good works, then we tend to be slightly boastful of those good works.

This was what happened in Jesus' story of the Pharisee and the tax collector. The Pharisee is boastful. 'God, I thank you that I am not like other people. . . .' That sentence could have made good sense. The Christian is not like other people. But the Pharisee went on to talk about the good things he had done: 'I fast . . . I pay tithes. . . .'

If salvation is by any kind of human achievement then we tend to boast in that achievement.

In Corinth some boasted of their high position in society or of their wisdom or cleverness. Paul says God chose 'foolish things . . . weak things . . . lowly things . . . things that are nothing . . . so that no person should boast before God' (1 Cor. 1:27–29). God has deliberately chosen that the way of salvation should not be by anything that men and women can boast about in themselves. Everything comes to us through Jesus alone. 'Let him who boasts boast in the Lord' (1 Cor. 1:31). Salvation is 'by grace' and 'through faith' and 'not as a result of works, so that no one should boast' (Eph. 2:8–9).

Jewish people tended to boast in their knowledge of the Mosaic law.

Paul has said this earlier. He spoke of those who 'rest in the law and boast in God'. People tended to boast in their nationality. 'We people have the law of God. We are the ones who have salvation. Now as for you gentiles . . . !'

There was something boastful and even racist in the way in
which they thought of themselves. Many are the same
today, especially when a religion or philosophy is identified
with one particular nation. 'Now we have this religion
. . .', 'Now we have this law . . .', they say. There is
something boastful about their very manner and tone of
voice.

In Philippians 3 one can hear an echo of how it was in
the life of Paul before he was saved. 'Circumcised on the
eighth day, of the people of Israel, of the tribe of Benjamin. . . .' Paul is looking back on his earlier life and
relating to us the way he used to feel about himself. 'I am
of the people of Israel!' he had said. 'I come from the tribe
of Benjamin,' he had affirmed with a haughty tone of
voice. But any way of feeling righteous that has any hint
of this kind of boastful spirit is certainly not the way of
salvation.

**God has so arranged things that the only way
of salvation there is totally excludes human
boastfulness.**

Everything Paul has said in verses 21–26 excludes boasting.
He has said that our only hope of salvation is to have a
righteousness that comes from outside of ourselves. In one
respect there is no difference between any person and any
other member of the human race. 'All have sinned.' This
excludes boasting. If all have sinned, what possibility is there
for one person to boast over another?

The sinfulness of the human race, says Paul, was so bad that it needed the atoning death of Jesus for us to have dealings with God. The death of Jesus was a sacrifice turning away the wrath of God. How can there be any room left for anyone to feel superior to any other person? When we see that God's anger was against us, so that it took the death of Jesus to turn God's wrath away, how can there be any boasting left? Then Paul has told us that we were saved through the redemption that was in Christ Jesus. This has let us know that we were in bondage. Everything Paul has said has excluded any possibility of boasting or self-confidence.

This means, then, that the only hope for any one of us is to come to God with no claims to any kind of righteousness. It is humbling, humiliating. I do not know that God wants us specially to grovel and pretend anything that we do not feel. We do not have to take part in any play-acting before God. But we do have to face facts. It is deeply humbling to realize that nothing in us can deserve salvation. The righteousness of Jesus comes wholly from outside of us. We stand before God entirely with a borrowed righteousness. Only if we see it this way have we really grasped hold of what constitutes the gospel of Jesus.

Boasting is excluded! It is shut out once and for ever. If we ever truly see the way Jesus is the one and only Saviour, we shall drop all of our little boastings in ourselves, all our pretended goodness, all our counterfeit righteousness. We shall stand before God as we really are and trust in Jesus as our only hope.

9

The Law of Faith (Romans 3:27)

Paul asks the question: what kind of law is it that excludes boasting? The true gospel, the one and only gospel, will not allow us to brag about anything in ourselves, The gospel excludes boasting. But then what kind of gospel is it? Boasting is excluded. 'By what law? By the law of works? No, by the law of faith' (Rom. 3:27).

After all that Paul has said, with great lucidity and clarity, it is surprising that we self-righteous human beings still seem to trip over Paul's teaching that we are righteous before God only through being given the righteousness of Jesus.

Paul is playing with words. He is using the word 'law' in a playful way. He says in effect: Do you want to be under a law? Well, what kind of law is it that will exclude human boastfulness? Will salvation-by-good-works exclude boasting? Of course not! Everyone who feels that they stand before God because they have done something good has a bit of boastfulness in them.

Human self-righteousness tends to corrupt the gospel.

Abraham had been right before God by trusting in the promises of God. But as time went on Abraham's descendants forgot how Abraham had started in his relationship with God. We are terribly self-righteous and proud. We like a 'gospel' or a 'religion' that allows us to retain some pride in our own achievements. We like to feel good about ourselves and be able to boast a little in what we have achieved! Righteousness-by-law-keeping fits in with human pride. Righteousness-by-our-good-works makes us feel that we have performed well. But Paul asks, what kind of law is it that will exclude this boastful self-righteousness of ours? Will obedience to some law demanding our good works exclude this human boastfulness? No, never!

Fears about holiness tend to corrupt the gospel.

The glorious teaching of Paul that we are justified simply by trusting in Jesus gets covered over and forgotten because people are worried that somehow salvation-by-grace does not produce holiness in us. Actually in the history of the church it has been when people have wanted to be holy by legalistic self-effort that they have fallen into sin! People who want to be saved by their own righteousness actually do not get to a very high level of godliness. They are not pure in heart, they do not hunger and thirst after righteousness.

When we know that we are saved totally by the righteousness of Jesus being given to us, we want to start living for him. We begin to want to be genuinely righteous in heart and in spirit.

Holiness starts when we abandon all attempts to be justified by any law at all. Holiness starts when we admit that we have no holiness of our own and have to be covered with the righteousness of Jesus. Our righteousness is never good enough for us to stand before God in ourselves. Even when we have been saved for ten years, twenty years, thirty years, we shall never be holy enough to stand before God in our own righteousness. Sometimes Christians get worried that somehow a hunger for holiness will be lost if we think that salvation is by grace alone. But salvation is by grace alone! Paul says so, with great clarity. True holiness begins when we admit we need the righteousness of Jesus.

Then Paul talks about a 'law of faith'. He is playing with the word 'law' and using it in the sense of 'principle', 'authoritative guideline'. What excludes boasting is when we live by faith – and more faith – and more faith still. The Christian life begins when we stand before God as a lawbreaker, as one who has displeased God. We believe what God says about us. Then we believe what God says about Jesus. We believe he has died for us. We believe we cannot save ourselves. We take it by faith that in Jesus there is redemption – deliverance from bondage. In Jesus there is propitiation – release from being under God's wrath. When we believe God's Word in this way we already have the Holy Spirit within us. Then we persist in faith. There is no room for boasting. We know that the habits of sin are deeply ingrained in us. But we believe! We are not living by a principle of being under some law like the Mosaic law or a law of our own inventing. We believe! We go on believing that Jesus will work in our hearts, that Jesus sees us and will enable purity within. We are rejoicing in the assurance of being totally covered by the righteousness of Jesus. We are rejoicing in the fact that we do not feel condemned. Jesus is our righteousness. In all of this, boasting is excluded. We live on the love of Jesus towards us. Any kind of holiness that is boastful is not holiness at all. There is a certain kind of person who does good in order to show off. He or she loves to draw attention to what is being done. This makes the other person feel bad. It makes the other one feel inferior. Jesus never did a thing like that. He was criticized because he would associate with wicked people and treat them as though they were his best friends.

Holiness is being like Jesus. It starts when we admit our sinfulness. We believe Jesus died for us on the cross to pay the price of our sinfulness. There is no room for boastfulness. We give our lives to him as a way of showing we believe he bought us on the cross. Then Jesus gives us his Spirit and we live the life of persistent faith in him. When we are honest with ourselves we know that we need the cleansing blood of Jesus every day. Where is the boasting? Is it excluded by salvation-by-law-keeping? No, it is excluded by faith in the blood of Jesus.

10

Justification without Works (Romans 3:28)

Paul asks the question: what kind of law is it that excludes boasting? The answer is 'the law of faith' (3:27). He explains, *For we reckon a person to be justified by faith without the works of the law* (Rom. 3:28). He is repeating what he has said in Romans 3:21–22a, but puts it even more clearly. We notice in passing that Paul uses the Greek word normally translated 'man' but obviously its meaning is 'person'; it includes women.

In this verse, Martin Luther, the German Reformer, used the translation 'justified by faith alone'. Strictly there is no 'alone' in the Greek. Yet Luther was within his rights to add a word to make the meaning clear. Translators are doing that all the time, to bring out the meaning of the original.

Boasting is excluded by the principle of faith because 'we reckon' something. There is a reference to thinking here. We are aware Jesus is our only hope of having an acceptable righteousness before God. We are conscious that our own good works are useless to justify us. It is this conscious awareness that only Jesus can be our righteousness that shuts out the possibility of boasting.

We have seen that justification means to be covered with the righteousness of Jesus (Ch. 3). It is a vitally important subject, and uses the language of a law court (Ch. 3). It presupposes the reality of sin and of God's wrath against it (Ch.3). We have seen the meaning of the word (Ch. 4) and the way we are justified so freely and generously (Ch. 4). We have noticed that justification takes place through the redemption and propitiation of the cross (Chs. 5–6). We have seen how it vindicates God (Ch. 7) and excludes boasting (Ch. 8). It puts down works and upholds faith (Ch. 9).

The foundational blessing of becoming and being a Christian is to be justified.

This is not an experience that we feel. It is not being made holy. It is not the same as being born again. It is not the gift of the Spirit. It is something that happens outside of us, when in the courts of heaven God declares that we are righteous in his sight because we are covered with the righteousness of Jesus Christ.

The means by which this blessing becomes ours is faith.

We look away from ourselves altogether. We cease to trust or hope for anything from ourselves, and we lean our trust on Jesus.

This being justified is 'without the works of the law'.

This means that we are not saved by any aspect of the law of Moses. We are not justified by becoming a Jew or by any aspect of the requirement laid upon Jewish people in the Mosaic law. It means that we are not saved by keeping the ten commandments or by righteous deeds of our own. It also means that our sins do not block justification.

The question is sometimes asked how Paul's teaching relates to James's teaching in James 2:24: 'By works a person is justified, and not by faith only.' The answer is that the word 'justify' in James does not refer to initial salvation. James uses the word to mean 'get approved by God after we have been saved'. We are 'justified' in Paul's sense by faith only. That is to say, we are declared righteous with Christ's righteousness by faith only. James agreed with this. He quoted the case of Abraham in James 2:23, 'Abraham believed God and that – just believing – 'was reckoned to him for righteousness'. James has the same doctrine as Paul. Like Paul he gets that doctrine from Genesis 15:6. He interprets Genesis 15:6 in the same way as Paul did. So far there is no difference between Paul and James at all.

There is a difference in how they use the word 'justify'. Paul uses 'justify' to mean 'having righteousness reckoned to us'. James believes in the same teaching about having righteousness reckoned to us but he does not use the word 'justify' in this connection.

James uses the word 'justify' in connection with something else. At least twenty years after Abraham was 'justified' in Paul's sense, he had come to a high level of godliness so that God was able to say, 'I know you fear me'. James uses 'justify' of that! James 2:21 says, 'Was not Abraham . . . justified by works when he offered up Isaac upon the altar' – and that was decades after he was 'reckoned righteous' by his faith in God's promise. There are decades of time between the events of Genesis 15:6 and Genesis 22. Abraham was justified, in Paul's sense of the word, by faith alone and that was the start of his life as one of God's true people. He was justified, in James's sense of the word, by works of faith that took place decades after the start of his life as one of God's true people.

We are reading Paul! Our theme at this point of Romans 3 is not how we may so live godly lives of faith that God declares he is pleased with us. Our concern is how we ever get to stand before God in the first place as accepted and acceptable to him. That is certainly a matter of 'faith only'.

We are boldly and daringly to forget ourselves altogether. We do not have to get to a certain level of mourning for our sins. We do not have to get to a certain level of amending our wicked ways. We are ungodly. We have failed to live up to God's will a thousand times and more. But we are believing in Jesus Christ. He is our only hope. We are nothing but failures. But Jesus was perfectly obeying the Father on the cross and he was perfectly bearing the penalty of sin. I can forget about myself altogether. I am trusting in Jesus. He is my righteousness. I reckon I am justified by Jesus' righteousness. I need nothing else.

11

A Gospel for All (Romans 3:29–30)

The first consequence of Paul's gospel in Romans 3:21–26 is that the gospel totally excludes boasting (3:27–28). Now Paul mentions a second consequence of what he has said: the gospel enables the message of salvation to be the same for the entire world.

Paul asks: *Or is God the God of Jews only?* (Rom. 3:29). If salvation comes by keeping the Mosaic law, then salvation would only be for Jews. Paul is insistent that the Mosaic law was given to Israel only. The Bible never supports the idea that gentiles somehow had the law of God. Romans 2:14–15 is sometimes quoted in this connection, but that certainly does not teach that gentiles had the law. That passage explicitly speaks of gentiles who did *not* have the law. I believe it refers to gentile Christians fulfilling the law by the Spirit. It is an anticipation of what Paul will say in Romans 8:1–13 and 13:8–10. It is true that gentiles have an instinctive knowledge of God's righteous requirement but the word 'law' is never used in this connection. People talk about 'natural law' but this is not Bible language. If salvation were by Mosaic legislation or by the commands given to Moses on Sinai it would exclude the gentiles. This is why the Mosaic law had to be 'abolished' (Eph. 2:15) before gentiles could become one with the people of God.

The law was a dividing wall of hostility. If salvation were by the law, and gentiles were without the law, then salvation by law-keeping would exclude gentiles. They would have to become Jews before they could be saved. That was precisely what the 'Judaizers' of New Testament times thought, but the apostles regarded that as entirely false.

So Paul goes on: *Is he not the God of gentiles also?* Then he answers his own question: *Yes, he is the God of gentiles also!* (Rom. 3:29). *This is because God is one, and he will justify the circumcised by faith and the uncircumcised through that same faith* (Rom. 3:30).

The arrival of Jesus Christ and the full manifestation of salvation in him abolishes the law. The law upheld a distinction between Jew and gentile. Jews were circumcised. The law was given to them only. It actually separated gentiles and Jews, and was intended to do so. Admittedly the extreme hatred that developed between Jew and gentile was not the intent of the law. Yet distinction and difference certainly was the aim of God. If salvation came through law-keeping the Jews would be in a superior position. But salvation-by-law was never God's intent. For salvation to be for everyone it has to come 'without the law'. In sending Jesus as the fulfilment of the law and abolishing the law for everyone who believes, God opened the way of membership of the people of God for every believer on an equal status. Every believer is equally saved and equally a member of the people of God, regardless of whether they are Jew or gentile.

God is one! God does not have a divided mentality towards the human race. He is not two gods, a god for Jews and a god for gentiles. Everything God does and is in relationship to the world reflects his oneness and his unity. He is one in his holiness. His radiating holiness views the entire world in the same way. He will not be judging part of the world in his holiness, but overlooking the sin of another part of the world. God is one!

God is one in his provision of salvation. There is one way to him. He does not have a number of different ways of saving people. 'There are many different ways to find God', says many a modern man or woman. 'There are many different roads to God', they say. This is quite wrong. When people travel 'many different roads' to God, they are in fact travelling 'many different roads' to many different gods! The Christian gospel is quite clear. There is one human race. There is one God. 'There is no difference' in the fact that all have sinned (Rom. 3:22b–23). There is one Saviour. There is one way of getting the salvation of that one-and-only Saviour. It is the way of rejecting law-keeping, the way of rejecting self-justifying 'good works'. The one-and-only way is simple trust in Jesus – plus nothing! Plus no one!

'There is salvation in no one else' (Acts 4:12). He is the way, the truth and the life. He said: 'No one comes to the Father except through me'.

This is why salvation has to be by faith only. If salvation came through something in us, only some people would get it. If it were for the clever, only the clever would get it. If it were for the moral, only those with moral will-power would qualify. If it were by a national law, only those of that nation would qualify. But salvation in Jesus has 'broken down the dividing wall' – the Mosaic law. It has put both Jew and gentile on a level by bringing to them the same way of salvation.

If men and women are without faith in Christ, they are totally without salvation. If they have Christ, they have heaven. If they lack Christ, they are still under the unappeased anger of God towards sin. Without the only Way there is no route to the Father. Without the only Truth men and women have no knowledge of themselves or of God. Without the only Life there is no purpose, no hope, no vitality, no future. God is one, and he will justify the circumcised by faith and the uncircumcised through that same faith. All men and women must come the same way. They must come by the 'sacrifice which turns away God's anger'. They must abandon for ever any hope that their keeping of the Mosaic law – or any other law – will help them in a personal relationship to God. If they have Christ they have everything.

12

Fulfilling the Law (Romans 3:31)

A third consequence of Paul's gospel is that it establishes the Mosaic law. *Do we therefore nullify the law through faith? Let it not be! On the contrary we establish the law* (Rom. 3:31). When Paul makes this assertion is he looking backwards or forwards? Is he expecting us to see from Chapters 1–3 that his gospel actually establishes the law? Or is he making a statement which he expects to demonstrate and prove in what follows in the forthcoming chapters? It is likely that he is doing both of these things. He has already said some things which ought to make us see that his message establishes the law.

Why does he ask this question, 'Do we therefore nullify the law through faith?' It is because much of what he has said might entice us into thinking, mistakenly, that Paul is disparaging the law of God. He has said that Jewish people who had the law were equally guilty before God as gentiles (2:1–29). The law concerning circumcision did not neces-sarily give the Jew any advantage over the gentile. Salvation is 'without the law' (3:21). Is Paul nullifying the law through this message about faith? Paul's answer is: the gospel is the fulfilling of the law. The law could easily be misused. The law could mistakenly be taken to mean that salvation was by works. It could give the impression that salvation required Jewish nationality. It could give the impression that it was a guide to holiness in one's personal relationship to God.

All of this would be a mistaken approach to the law. Salvation is not by any works, certainly not by the works done in fulfilment of the Mosaic legislation. Salvation does not require Jewish nationality. The law does not help as a guide to personal holiness in a direct relationship to God.

Yet Paul is not brushing aside the law. Everything he has been saying actually establishes the law. It was what the law was pointing to all the time. The word 'law' here refers to the entire Mosaic system. Yet it includes the writings that were known to come largely from that time, the 'books of Moses'. What would trouble Jewish readers is Paul's apparent disparagement of the entire ministry of Moses. Although 'the law' includes the tenth commandment, Paul does not refer only to a developed version of the ten commandments, extended to include the desires of the heart. It is everything that came in the time of Moses, including Moses' book of Genesis.

1. Paul has been establishing the law by insisting the entire human race is guilty before God. Paul insisted that the entire human race was under condemnation and under God's wrath. In the case of the gentiles their plight was obviously in the story of their progressive degradation (Rom. 1:18–32). In the case of Israel their condemnation was just as great but it was a condemnation that arose because of their breaking the Mosaic law. This is in fact 'fulfilling' the law. The law was intended to intensify knowledge of sin. When it gets broken its purpose is being established. The exasperated plight of the

Jew is what the law was intended to bring about. His indictment of Israel is establishing the law.

2. Paul has been establishing the law by bringing forward the blood of Jesus as the redemption of the world. This is what the law pointed forward to. The entire Mosaic system was riddled with symbolism that taught that relationship with God comes only by redemption through blood. Paul believes the gospel of Jesus is the fulfilment of this symbol- ism. Is the law nullified by a message of faith in atoning blood? Not at all! That was precisely what the law was pointing to. The gospel establishes everything the law was saying.

3. Paul has been establishing the law by a message that excludes boasting. 'The law shuts every mouth and excludes all boasting' (Rom. 3:19,20). The gospel comes in and ratifies the very thing that the law does. It doubly excludes boasting and so establishes the law.

However all of this is looking back to what Paul has already said. There is reason to think Paul is also looking forward to what he will say. Elsewhere in Romans, when Paul asks a question and then says, 'May it not be!' he is looking forward. When in Chapters 6:1, 6:15, 7:7 and 7:13 he says, 'May it not be!' in each case he shows what he means in what follows. Paul frequently raises objections and then answers them in his following words (see also Rom. 3:1,5,7–8,9; 8:31; 9:6a,14,19,30; 11:1,7). This means that although something of what he means by 'establishing the law' is already clear, he has not finished yet and he intends to show even more fully how his gospel establishes the law.

4. Paul establishes the law by reminding his readers that Genesis is also in 'the law'. Paul goes on to deal with Abraham in Romans 4:1–5,9–25. 'The law' is the Mosaic system but the 'books of Moses' include Genesis! The story of the law could not overthrow the story about Abraham, also in the law! 'Tell me, you who want to be under the law', said Paul in Galatians 4:21, 'do you not hear the law?' And he went on to talk about Abraham! 'For it is written that Abraham had two sons. . . .' (Gal. 4:22). The Mosaic legislation was never intended to overthrow the earlier message of salvation already to be found in the story of Abraham's faith and justification which was recorded in the 'books of Moses'. Paul is about to demonstrate from one of the books of Moses – Genesis – that justification is by faith.

5. Paul establishes the law by arguing that the life of the Holy Spirit is the surest way to fulfilling what the law is pointing to. This will be his point in Romans 8:4, developed in Romans 8:5–17.

6. Paul establishes the law by arguing that the one command concerning love establishes everything that the law was intended to bring to the lives of Israelite people. This will be his point in Romans 13:8–10.

13

The Case of Abraham (Romans 4:1–3)

Romans 4 is not a major new section. Paul has put to his readers all of the basic points concerning his message of justification (3:21–31), but he has still not quite finished what he wants to say. In Romans 4 Paul now does five things. He shows that this way of salvation that he has put before us was the way in which Abraham was justified (Rom. 4:1–5), and it was the way in which David was justified (4:6–8). In other words Romans 4:1–8 confirms and backs up what Paul has already said in Romans 1.2 and Romans 3:21. The gospel was predicted in the Old Testament.

Then in Romans 4:9–12 Paul explains how this gospel relates to the law of circumcision that was given to Israel in the days of Moses.

Next Paul argues that the goal of our salvation ('inheritance') is not reached through law-keeping but is reached through this 'righteousness of faith' that he has referred to. He puts this to us in a section that runs from Romans 4:13 until about the middle of verse 17. Then in the middle of verse 17 Paul begins to describe what this faith was actually like as it worked out in Abraham's life and laid hold of the inheritance that God has promised to Abraham. He goes on in this line until the end of verse 21. Then in the last lines of this section, he explains that the faith which inherited blessing was the very same faith which brought Abraham's justification in the first place (4:22). It is this kind of faith in a risen Jesus which brings our justification also (Rom. 4:23–25).

Abraham is the 'father' of all believers: every main ingredient in the life of faith can be found in the story of Abraham. At the end of the chapter Paul makes the point that what was written about Abraham applies to the Christian in his day and in our day (4:23–25).

He introduces the subject by asking a question: *What then shall we say that Abraham, our forefather according to the flesh, has found?* (Rom. 4:1). 'Flesh' in Romans 4:1 has the meaning 'human nature, human descent' (as in Rom. 1:3; elsewhere it has other meanings). The question Paul asks is: what was Abraham's way of salvation? How did he get to be righteous before God? Was it his godliness? Or his circumcision? Or what?

Why does Paul expound his convictions by using the story of Abraham? There are several reasons.

1. Paul is convinced that God has deliberately put for-ward Abraham as the model of how we are justified; this is his point in Romans 4:23–25.

2. Jewish people admired Abraham, yet they seemed to admire Moses even more. Actually Abraham is more foun-dational than Moses. The people of Israel tended to make too much of Moses. Moses was their great law-giver. But actually Abraham was earlier than Moses and came to experience salvation without in any way knowing about the law of Moses. Paul wants to help Jewish people. They

had come to believe that salvation was by law-keeping and that Abraham was a great law-keeper. In speaking of Abraham's 'salvation' we must remember that it was at a pre-Christian level. I do not think Abraham had the fullness of the gift of the Spirit. However he did have 'justification' and this is the basic ingredient of 'salvation'.

3. Paul wants to show that the gospel is not new. The gospel was taught in the Old Testament (see also 1:2; 3:21).

4. Paul wants to shut out any kind of boasting or self-reliance with regard to salvation. Verse 2 has some- times been taken as if it meant that Abraham could boast, so long as he were not boasting before God. This takes it as if it said: 'For if Abraham was justified by works, he does have something to boast about, but not before God, only before other people!' But this would seem to contradict Romans 3.27. God does not want us boasting at all about our achieving salvation by our good work, not to anyone! It is better to take verse 2b as a compressed statement with the sense, 'But this is not possible before God!' So Paul says, *For if Abraham were justified by works he had something to boast about. But this is not possible before God!* (Rom. 4:2). The word 'boast' is taking up the theme of 3:27. Could someone as great as Abraham perhaps be in a position to boast? Justification by works always leads to pride. It may be a subtle matter but it is always there. Paul answers: 'But this is not possible before God!' Even Abraham is not able to boast in his righteousness before God. Those who try to justify themselves have forgotten that it is God who sets the standards. 'If you, LORD, should mark iniquities, O Lord, who could stand?' (Ps. 130:3). 'Do not enter into

judgment with your servant', said the psalmist. 'For in your sight no person living is righteous' (Ps. 143:2).

Paul goes on to prove his point and answer his own question: *For what does the Scripture say? – Abraham believed God and it was reckoned to him for righteousness* (Rom. 4:3). He quotes Genesis 15:6. The Old Testament had supreme authority for Paul and his Jewish friends. It clinches the argument. To show how Abraham was saved Paul simply refers his readers to the book of Genesis.

How and when did Abraham get right with God? It was not after his life of obedience. In Genesis 12:3 Abraham is told one of his descendants will bring world-wide blessing. It is repeated in Genesis 15. Abraham is given a tiny glimpse of the coming of Christ. He believed the promise, and God declared him righteous. God treated him as a righteous person. Abraham was saved simply by believing the promise about Jesus! There is only one way of salvation. Abraham was saved in the same way we are saved. He believed God's promise.

14

Justifying the Ungodly (Romans 4:1–5)

Paul's example of Abraham confirms much of what he said in 3:21–31. 'Abraham believed God, and it was reckoned to him as righteousness.'

The story of Abraham confirms that salvation is a matter of grace.

Abraham was from a pagan land. There was no 'holy nation' of Israel when Abraham was called by God. Abraham's family came from Ur of the Chaldees. Then they moved to Haran. These two towns were centres of moon-worship according to modern archaeological scholars. Abraham certainly was not blessed by God because of his Israelite nationality. Joshua said, 'Your fathers lived a long time ago beyond the river Euphrates . . . and they served other gods. And I took Abraham . . . ' (Josh. 24:2). God simply stepped into Abraham's life. There were no pre-liminaries. The first time we hear of any relationship between God and Abraham it is a case of God's stepping into his life. It confirms Paul's point. 'They are justified, as a gift, by his grace.'

The story of Abraham confirms that salvation comes by faith, by trusting God's promise.

The first time we hear of any relationship between God and Abraham, God speaks to him. God comes to him with a speech full of promises: 'I will . . . I will . . . I will . . .' (Gen. 12:1–3). God gives Abraham a string of things that he will do. He points Abraham to the number of stars and says, 'So shall your seed be' (Gen. 15:5). Abraham believes God. This is all that is involved. Abraham is not said to be a specially godly person, nor was he circumcised, nor was he at that time a Jew. There was only one thing Abraham did. Abraham believed God!

The story of Abraham confirms that salvation comes by being given a righteousness that is not our own.

It is not that righteousness was worked into Abraham's heart and life; that came later. What happened at the point mentioned in Genesis 15:6 was that righteousness was 'reckoned' or 'counted' as being his. This confirms Paul's point earlier that salvation is a matter of being clothed or covered by a righteousness that is not ours, and that this righteousness comes entirely from God.

The story of Abraham confirms that salvation is by faith alone: no human contribution is made.

Abraham was not specially godly. He was not even asked to show any godliness before Genesis 17. He was 'justified' before God called him to holiness of life. Paul has argued that we are justified exclusively by the blood and righteous-ness of Christ and not at all by how well we are doing in obedience. The case of Abraham proves the point.

The story of Abraham confirms that salvation is for gentiles.

One could almost say that Abraham was a gentile at the time. He came from a pagan area. He was uncircumcised.

The story of Abraham confirms that salvation is not an invention of Paul or even of Jesus.

Paul is writing specially to help Jewish Christians. There were Jewish people who thought that Jesus or Paul were bringing some startlingly new religion. But this is not true at all. 'Don't think that I have come to destroy the law and the prophets' said Jesus. 'I am not coming to destroy them. I am the one that they refer to. I am coming to fulfil them.' Abraham was justified in the same way we are justified.

Being justified was the way people were able to relate to God centuries before Jesus came.

The story of Abraham confirms that salvation is without the law.

The law of God given in the days of Moses did not exist in Abraham's time. By 'the law' I mean not only the ten commandments, but the entire Mosaic law. Salvation is not by means of the morality of the law, not by means of the tabernacle worship of the law, not by means of the require- ment of circumcision, without the keeping of holy days, without regulations about food. None of these regulations of the law existed. The case of Abraham confirms what Paul had said in Romans 3:28. 'For we reckon a person to be justified by faith without the works of the law.'

The story of Abraham confirms that salvation comes in a way that excludes boasting.

Earlier Paul was asking, 'Where then is the boasting?' and he said that the gospel totally excluded any form of boasting in one's achievement. If salvation is by good works, then we tend to be boastful of those good works. Abraham's story proves the point. Salvation is 'by grace' and 'through faith' and 'not as a result of works, so that no one should boast' (Eph. 2:8,9). In the story of Abraham we see again that God has arranged things concerning salvation in a way that totally excludes human boastfulness. The true gospel, the one-and-only gospel, will not allow us to brag about anything in ourselves.

The next two verses put very sharply the freedom of the gospel. *Now to the one who works the reward is not reckoned according to grace but according to debt* (Rom. 4:4), *but to the one who does not work but believes upon the one who justifies the ungodly, that person's faith is reckoned as righteousness* (Rom. 4:5). The person is ungodly, does not do anything, believes – and he or she is right with God! Paul actually says we are saved by doing nothing!

Paul wants us to see the difference between working for something and receiving it as a gift. Paul uses the illustration of a workman. It is not optional to give wages but a matter of obligation. The employer has to 'Render . . . that which is just and equal' (Col. 4:1). If salvation is by works then it comes into the realm of wages. It is a matter of duty, obligation. It would be entirely outside of the realm of grace.

But Abraham was saved by doing nothing. Romans 4:5 is the strongest statement of justification in the Bible. We come as ungodly people. We believe. And we are clothed with God's righteousness.

15

Another Gospel? (Romans 4:1–5)

Romans 4:4,5 puts very plainly to us the fact that justification is effortless. It is shockingly free. The scandal of the gospel is that we are justified by doing nothing! The person is ungodly, does not do anything, believes – and he or she is right with God! The starting point, the basis, of our salvation is startlingly free and generous. True, we shall have to work out our salvation with works of faith. But the foundation, the rock on which we stand, our assurance of acceptance with God, is totally free, absolutely unconditional, instantly assuring and immediately merciful to us. Throughout the centuries there has always been a tendency to move away from this amazing joy of knowing that we are saved 'without the law'.

Some have confused justification and godliness.

Some friends seem to think that God accepts us because of how good we are or because we have given our lives to Jesus. Not at all! We are not accepted by God because we have given our lives to Jesus. We are accepted because we are clothed with the righteousness of Christ.

In Roman Catholic thinking we are justified by being made righteous. The idea is that by our faith, our love, our good works and our baptism we are 'made righteous' and accepted by God. But this is not the gospel! It is nearer to the teaching of Paul's enemies than to the teaching of Paul. In being justified, the righteousness that covers us is God's righteousness. It is not our love or our good works. It is not our righteousness; we are clothed in someone else's righteousness.

In our being justified the 'channel' of our being given a righteousness is our trusting Jesus. The means of salvation is faith. Jesus alone is the Saviour. Our faith is simply our receiving what he has done for us. Nothing else comes into it. Baptism is not the way of salvation. Our love of God is not the way of justification. It is only a matter of receiving Jesus and being covered by his righteousness.

There have been those who want to say that Paul is not attacking the righteousness of the law but is only dealing with the abuse of the law.

One version of this teaching goes like this.

> The problem of Israel was not legalism; it was nationalism. Salvation *is* by works, but not by works of Jewish nationalism. All Paul is doing in Romans and Galatians is arguing against the idea that we have to keep the law as a mark of Jewish identity. By 'works of the law' Paul means Jewish cultural 'identity-markers'.

One New Testament scholar wanted to translate Galatians 2:16 'A person is not justified by the works of the law *except* through faith' (that is, we have faith and then we *are* justified by the law!).

On all of this I have three comments.

All people everywhere tend to think salvation is by good works.

Some scholars argue that the Judaism of Paul's day was not legalistic so either Paul was wrong or our interpretation of Paul is wrong. But then many New Testament scholars are more like Paul's enemies than they are like Paul! The truth is, all religions, all people everywhere including New Testament scholars tend to think that somehow our godliness has to contribute to our justification. Romans 4:4–5 is a follow-up of Romans 3:21–31. Clearly Romans 4:4–5 is not arguing just against Jewish 'identity-markers' (they did not exist in Abraham's day). Paul is arguing against any kind of justification by any kind of 'good works'.

Paul's phrase 'the works of the law' refers to every part of the law, not merely to Jewish 'identity-markers'.

A thorough study of Romans 3:27–4:8, Romans 9:30–10:8 and Philippians 3:2–11 shows clearly that 'the works of the law' is a reference not only to Jewish identity-markers but also to the morality of the law. Paul himself had once boasted in his good works and not just in his Jewishness.

The case of Abraham shows that 'works' and 'works of the law' are the same thing in Paul's mind. When Paul is writing with the law in mind, he uses the term 'works of the law'. When he has Abraham in mind, the law did not exist, so he has to use the phrase 'works' (Rom. 4:2). He does the same thing when writing to a gentile church like that of Ephesus ('not of works', Eph. 2:9).

The term 'the law' does not mean 'legalistic abuse of the law'.

It means 'the law'! When Paul says we are justified 'without the law' (Rom. 3:21), it does not mean 'without a legalistic abuse of the law'. The next phrase refers to 'the law and the prophets'. 'The law' clearly refers to the first five books of the Bible, especially the Mosaic legislation. There is no place in the New Testament where 'law' means 'legalistic abuse of the law'. Paul refers to a particular time when 'the law came in' (Rom. 5:13). It refers to the days of Moses. Galatians 3:13 does not mean 'Christ redeemed us from the curse of a wrong use of the law.'

Modern ways of moving away from the gospel are subtle. No longer are we so bothered about medieval catholicism. But the modern 'clever' versions of justification by works are no different in principle from what Paul was arguing against. In his day, it was the Judaizers. Later it was medieval catholicism. Nowadays it is 'covenantal nomism' (to use the scholars' jargon). But it all comes to the same thing: salvation by works!

But justification is by faith in Jesus, without the works of any law. It is by the righteousness of Christ being reckoned as ours. The Mosaic law is abolished for the Christian. We fulfil its righteousness by walking in the Spirit. It is still true: 'To the one who works the reward is not reckoned according to grace but according to debt, but to the one who does not work but believes upon one who justifies the ungodly, his faith is reckoned as righteousness.'

16

The Case of David (Romans 4:6–8)

Paul is showing us that the way of justification that he has
put before us (in 3:21–31) was foreshadowed by the way
in which Abraham was justified (Rom. 4:1–5). Now,
before he develops his argument he spends a few sentences
arguing that the case of David is similar. Abraham is not
an exceptional case. David was also 'declared righteous'
without works.

*Just as also David speaks of the blessedness of the person to
whom God reckons righteousness without works* (Rom. 4:6),
*Blessed are those whose transgressions are forgiven, and whose sins
are covered* (Rom. 4:7). *Blessed is the man whose sin the Lord
does not reckon* (Rom. 4:8).

Paul is quoting from Psalm 32 which (as the title of the
psalm tells us) was a psalm of David. It was obviously
written at a time when David had committed some sin.
There is a lot of confession of sin in it. 'I acknowledged my
sin to you,' says David.

One can see why Paul chose this particular psalm. It
contains the same matters that he has already been putting
before the Christians at Rome.

Salvation is a matter of what is 'reckoned'.

The reason Paul quotes this psalm is because it has the word 'reckon' in it. David is sinful in himself. Apparently he had recently fallen into sin. Yet he knows that he has been forgiven. The basis upon which he has been forgiven is that God will 'reckon' something other than what he is in and of himself. This is precisely Paul's teaching. God 'reckons' us righteous when we trust in Jesus. We may not be righteous in ourselves, but God justifies even the ungodly!

David's salvation was 'without works'.

David was clearly not righteous in himself. David makes no claim on God. He makes no claim to be worthy. He admits his sinfulness in this psalm. He speaks of transgressions and sins but he does not speak of anything good he has done. He is not looking to his own good works.

David is able to stand before God despite his sin.

He has sinned, yet he is still praying. He still has contact with God. How is this? He is standing in a God-given righteousness. Despite all the sin that David has to confess he is still saved. He is able to come into the presence of God in prayer.

His standing before God is a matter of faith.

The law existed in David's day but David is not quoting it
or referring to it at all. His praying is by faith. David has
turned to the Lord, and is trusting him no matter what he
has done. He finds his refuge against sin and guilt in God.
'You are my hiding place', he says (Ps. 32:7).

David is enjoying the experience of being forgiven.

Forgiveness is negative. Justification is positive. But they
are closely related. The point is that he was forgiven
without works.

He knows that people are blessed if their 'transgressions
are forgiven' and their 'sins are covered' because he can say
about himself, 'Blessed is the man whose sin the Lord does
not reckon.' Forgiveness is a wonderful thing. What relief
of conscience has come to David. Being 'righteous without
the law' brings us peace of conscience.

How is it that Paul can quote a psalm speaking of
forgiveness, when his precise concern is justification? It is
because there is no forgiveness without justification. Forgiveness is not a once-for-ever matter. Forgiveness has to
be received again and again. If we confess our sins, God
forgives us.

But the question is: how can we be forgiven? Paul's
answer is: David knew that there was a righteousness
available from God. David knew that forgiveness came to

him by his resting in the righteousness of another, of God himself.

To understand that we are forgiven by being covered by God's righteousness is a wonderful thing.

1. It brings peace of conscience. It means that we can relax. We do not have to be wondering whether God accepts us. David knew about 'righteousness' being reckoned. He had a long battle to confess he was a sinner at all, but when finally he rested in God's 'reckoning' him righteous, blessedness came into his life.

2. There is no need to struggle with feelings of what we deserve or what we do not deserve. It is very humbling but we look away from ourselves altogether.

3. There is assurance of forgiveness for us. If our forgiveness depends on our own deeds would we never feel strong enough or good enough or repentant enough to feel safe? But if we are resting in the righteousness of God himself we can have immediate assurance.

4. There is forgiveness despite great sins. We do not know what David had done, but by the sound of his description in Psalm 32 it was something serious. All manner of sins and wickedness can be forgiven by the blood of Jesus Christ.

What is of particular interest in this psalm is that David is writing at a time long after he first came to know God. David knew God as a young boy, looking after the sheep in the fields of Bethlehem. But now he is writing as a mature man, as a king and leader of Israel.

This is an important point. We never outgrow justification by faith. When we have been Christians for half a century we shall still be standing before God in the right-eousness he gave us as much as we were on the day we first came to know him. We shall never stand before God in any other way than the way we discovered at first. We can never outgrow the righteousness of Christ.

17

Justification and Circumcision
(Romans 4:9–10)

The next question Paul approaches is: how does salvation relate to circumcision? Jewish people often thought that salvation was a matter of being attached to the nation of Israel. If you were a Jew you were saved! Circumcision was the mark of being a Jew. It was the means of entry into the nation of Israel. So every Jewish man was circumcised and he tended to think of circumcision as the sign and guarantee of salvation.

Precisely the same misunderstanding is often found among those who grow up in 'Christian' nations or 'Christian' parts of the world. Jewish people often thought that circumcision was a sign of salvation and so if they were circumcised they were God's saved people. They were acting as if circumcision in itself brought salvation. People in Christianized areas or communities sometimes regard baptism or church member-ship in the same way. It is this kind of confusion that Paul addresses in Romans 4:9–12. He first of all raises the question: *Is this blessedness then upon the circumcision or upon the uncircum-cision, for we are saying 'Faith was reckoned to Abraham for righteousness'* (Rom. 4:9). According to Genesis 15:6 he was 'reckoned righteous'. But what exactly was it that brought this justification? How did circumcision fit in?

Paul answers by asking them to notice the order of events in Genesis. *How then was it reckoned to him? Was it while he was in circumcision or while he was in uncircumcision?* (Rom. 4:10a). At what stage in Abraham's life did he get this 'reckoned' righteousness from God? He answers: *It was not when he was circumcised. It was when he was uncircumcised* (Rom. 4:10b).

Paul says: you seem to think that it is circumcision that saves the Jew. But if you will remember, Abraham was said to be justified before he was ever circumcised. He was justified at the point mentioned in Genesis 15:6. The point where he was circumcised was some time later (Gen. 17:26). We know for sure that Abraham was justified without being circumcised.

Paul is arguing from sheer history. It is a fact that Abraham was justified without circumcision and before circumcision. This same kind of argument can be applied to modern equivalents. One can argue from the personal history of people who undoubtedly experience God's salvation.

Think of it in connection with baptism. There are many who seem to think that one receives salvation through baptism. There are sections of the professing church who teach this with differing degrees of clarity – or I should say varying degrees of puzzling obscurity. Even Bible-believing Christians can say things like, 'Baptism effectively conveys what God promises in the gospel'. The confusion comes in largely because anyone who thinks the word 'baptism' always refers to water-baptism is bound to end up with a doctrine of salvation-by-baptism. And it will be hard to fit it in with salvation by faith. Some people have been baptized but do not believe. Are they saved? Some will believe but not be baptized (mistakenly!) or will not get baptized for many years (again, mistakenly). Are such people saved or not? Would a person be lost if he or she did not believe? (Yes!) Would a person be lost if he or she were not baptized? (No!)

But one can argue in precisely the same way in which Paul argued with regard to Abraham and salvation. It is possible to know that one has experienced salvation. It is possible to know that one has received the Holy Spirit. It is possible to experience the Spirit of adoption in whom we cry 'Abba Father', and to experience the witness of the Holy Spirit. So one can ask Paul's question: how then was it experienced?

There are many people around who have experienced salvation before they ever 'went to church' or became church members or were baptized. It happened to me. I was brought up in a fairly pagan home. As a teenager I found Christ as my Saviour. Apart from a few weddings and funerals I had never been to church in my life. Is salvation by church involvement? Ask the people who have experienced salvation! Ask them Paul's question. How then was it reckoned? How then was it experienced? In a state of circumcision or in a state of uncircumcision? In a state of church-membership or in a state of un-church-membership?

There are many people who have experienced salvation long before they were baptized. Is salvation conveyed in the sacraments? Turn to the saved. Turn to those in Acts 10. Ask them: how did you receive salvation? How did you receive the Spirit? Was it in connection with baptism? They will tell you. 'No, not at all. We were gentile people. We had not been baptized and knew nothing about the church. But Peter the apostle was sent to us. He preached to us about Jesus (Acts 10:34–43). We already had faith in the God of Israel but we never knew much about Jesus. As Peter was preaching we knew in our hearts that we were hearing the Word of God. Suddenly God poured out on us his Holy Spirit' (Acts 10:44,45). 'Although we had never been circumcised that is what happened. We found ourselves rejoicing in God and worshipping him with the gift of tongues. All this happened before we were baptized with water. Only after this had happened to us did it occur to anyone that we ought to get baptized with water'.

It is a good way of arguing. Paul uses the same argument in Galatians 3:2: 'Did you receive the Spirit by the works of the law or by the hearing with faith?'

We can use the same logic in a hundred situations. How did the blessing come? By law? By ceremony? By circumcision? By baptism? How? The answer will normally be: by faith and by faith alone. Certainly that is how justification takes place: by faith in Jesus, and by faith alone!

18

The Seal of Salvation (Romans 4:11a)

Salvation did not come to Abraham by the ceremony of circumcision. It was a sheer historical fact that his being declared righteous was independent of his being circumcised. He was uncircumcised at the time God justified him. Similarly, for many Christians it is a sheer fact that their experience of salvation did not come by baptism.

But then one might ask: what is circumcision for? If circumcision does not automatically save what is its purpose?

Paul answers: *And he received the sign of circumcision as a seal of the righteousness of faith which he had while uncircumcised* (Rom. 4:11a).

Circumcision was a sign.

It was a sign of new life. In Genesis 17 Abraham receives a new name. He is made a new person, given a new enablement. Circumcision is a sign of what has happened to Abraham after he had been declared righteous. This is also the way in which the term is used later in the story of Israel.

It was also a sign that the promises of salvation would come through Abraham's line. Abraham and Sarah were miraculously given God's strength to conceive and bring to birth the miracle child Isaac. From this beginning the Saviour would come in the line of Abraham. This is why a Jewish boy was circumcised at birth. As soon as he was born he was a member of the people in whose line the Saviour would come. You only had to be born in Abraham's line to be the 'seed of Abraham' in a national-istic sense, although this did not mean you were the 'seed of Abraham' in the sense of having his salvation. Circum-cision was a sign of new birth, and a sign of the coming Saviour. It summoned Abraham to new obedience. Be-cause he was a new person a new obedience was expected of him.

Circumcision was a seal.

A seal is a way of making something secure and certain. Pilate 'sealed' the tomb of Jesus to make sure no one would tamper with it. 'Make it as sure as you can', said Pilate. 'So they . . . made the tomb sure, sealing the stone . . . ' (Matt. 27:64,65).

Circumcision was a seal of the salvation that Abraham had previously received. God came to Abraham and gave him something he did not have before. Circumcision said in effect to Abraham: 'I have accepted you as righteous. You are mine. You are justified because you have believed my word. The way in which you were saved is the way in which all of your spiritual children will be saved.' God was 'sealing' Abraham's salvation. He was making it doubly clear to Abraham that he was truly one who belonged to God and had God's salvation.

It is important to realize that circumcision was not a 'seal' to anyone other than Abraham. Paul says: 'he received . . . circumcision as a seal of the righteousness of faith which *he* had . . . '. 'Which *he* had!' It did not say to Abraham that all of his line would be saved. It said that *he* was saved and others would be saved if they followed him in his faith. When Abraham's children were circumcised it did not seal *their* salvation. It simply reminded them of the way Abraham was justified.

What is the equivalent of this in the Christian life? Is it water-baptism? Like circumcision, water-baptism is a 'sign' but it should not be described as a 'seal'. No one has his or her salvation made infallibly sure and certain by their being baptized in water.

The 'seal' of the Christian's salvation is the Holy Spirit. Remember the meaning of the word 'seal'. It refers to something that secures or makes absolutely certain. When Abraham was given circumcision it was an absolute guarantee of his salvation. It made him a hundred per cent certain that he was justified. The equivalent of this in the Christian life is the experiential receiving of the Holy Spirit. What gives us an absolute certainty of our salvation is the Spirit's being given to us in such a way that he is a seal to us of our salvation. The sealing of the Spirit not only means that our salvation is made sure by the presence of the Holy Spirit. It also means that we ourselves have a consciousness of our salvation. Ephesians 1:13 says, 'In Christ also, you people, having heard the Word of truth, the gospel of your salvation, and having believed in him, you were sealed by the Holy Spirit of promise.'

This 'seal' of the Holy Spirit makes the person sure of his or her salvation. Not only is salvation sure in itself. It is sure in the receiver's own consciousness, for Paul went on in Ephesians 1:14 to say that the seal of the Holy Spirit 'is the part-payment of our inheritance'. It is a little bit of our heavenly reward until we get to the whole of our heavenly reward. The Holy Spirit is 'the part-payment of our inheritance until the redemption of the possession'.

Circumcision did not 'seal' the salvation of the people of Israel. It was only a sign of how Abraham was saved and how anyone else can be saved, by faith in Jesus the seed of Abraham.

Water-baptism does not 'seal' the salvation of baptized people in general. It is a sign of the gospel but it does not seal anyone's salvation.

The seal of Abraham's salvation was the fact that God came to him, personally and individually, and on the occasion of his circumcision assured him of his personal salvation.

The seal of the individual Christian's salvation is the Holy Spirit. Water-baptism tells us and everyone else to believe in Jesus. If we do believe and God pours out the Spirit upon us, then we have the seal of our salvation. But the seal for us is not the water: it is the Spirit. And as there was a time gap between Abraham's justification and Abraham's sealing, there is a difference and there may be a time gap between our justification and our being sealed in our experience with the Holy Spirit.

19

The Father of Believers (Romans 4:11–12)

Paul explains that circumcision was not a way of salvation. It sealed the salvation that Abraham already had, and it pointed his descendants to the way of salvation, but it did not in itself automatically save anyone.

Why did God do things in precisely this way? Verses 11b–12 tell us. *The purpose was that Abraham might be the father of all those who believe in order to have righteousness reckoned to them, but without being circumcised* (Rom. 4:11b), *and the father of those circumcised people who not only are circumcised but also follow in the steps of the faith that Abraham our father had before he was circumcised* (Rom. 4:12).

This is a long and complicated sentence. Its logic can be laid out like this:

'The purpose was:

that Abraham might be the father of

1. all those who believe in order to have righteousness reckoned to them, but without being circumcised (Rom. 4:11b),
2. those circumcised people who not *only* are circumcised but *also* follow in the steps of the faith that Abraham our father had before he was circumcised'.

In other words God's purpose was that Abraham might
be the father of all believers. There are two groups of
believers. There are gentile believers who have faith in Jesus
but never were circumcised. And there are Jewish believers
who are circumcised but have come to faith.

It does not mean that Abraham is the father of Christians
and of Jewish people whether they believed or not! Rather
Abraham is the father of all believers, gentile and Jewish.
There was a stage when he was a believer but uncircumcised. There was a stage when he was a believer and
circumcised. He is the father of every kind of believer. But
the important thing is faith. It does not matter whether you
are in faith-plus-circumcision or faith-minus-circumcision.
The one who saves is Jesus, and what links on to him and
his salvation is faith.

There is only one people of God.

Jewish Christians and gentile Christians are all in one
spiritual family. They are all spiritually children of Abraham
because they have the same faith as Abraham.

Natural descent is not very important.

It does not matter that some people have Abraham as their
physical ancestor. What links us on to Jesus' salvation is
faith, not ancestry. The way to be a true child of Abraham
is to believe in the Lord Jesus Christ. Those who have the

faith of Abraham are the true seed of Abraham (see Gal. 3:6,7,9,29). Jewish people are the 'seed of Abraham' in a physical manner, but this aspect of things is not spiritually important. No saving blessing comes from God along lines of physical descent. There may be certain privileges to being connected to God's people but those privileges do not include automatic salvation.

Abraham is a spiritual model for every believer.

He is a model in what did not save him. His background did not save him. He descended from pagan people (Josh. 24:2). No Christian is saved because of his forebears. Abraham was not saved by circumcision. Equally no Christian is saved by circumcision or by any other religious ceremony. Abraham was not saved by good works. There is no mention of any good works in the early stages of Abraham's life. The fact that Abraham was uncircumcised at the point where he was reckoned tells us and everyone else to believe in Jesus. If we also believe and God pours out the Spirit upon us, then our receiving the Spirit makes it quite clear that faith was the means of salvation.

Abraham is a model in that he was saved without the involvement of the law. There was no Mosiac law in the days of Abraham. He was not taught by the law, was not under the godliness of the law, and was not convicted by the Mosaic law.

Abraham is a model for us in that he was justified through

faith and through faith only. His faith consisted in believing promises about his own seed, the line that led to Jesus. Without knowing the name Jesus, he was exercising faith in promises concerning Jesus. Abraham is in fact the major model of justification in the Bible. This is quite deliberate on God's part. He intended that Abraham should be the prototype for all time of the way of salvation.

Abraham is a model in that his faith led him to a high level of obedience without the Mosaic law. The obedience of Genesis 22 was the result of persistent faith. He is not only a model of salvation without the law. He is also a model of godliness without the law.

Abraham was a model of how faith works its way through to godliness. He was a model of patience. He had to endure many troubles and endure God's delays before he fulfilled his life's calling.

Abraham was a model of contentment. The major part of his inheritance lay beyond the grave. He was promised the entire land of Israel but when Sarah died did not have a patch of land he could call his own to bury his wife in. He was content to be a temporary resident in this world looking for a city beyond the grave (see Heb. 11:9,10).

He was a model in his persistence. He left Ur, in the land of Mesopotamia, trusting the promises of God. When he was driven by famine into Egypt he strayed from God's will but eventually got back to fellowship and communion with God. No matter what came his way he went on believing. Faith was the channel of salvation. Faith led him into heights of godliness. He was deliberately designed by God to be 'the father of us all' (Rom. 4:16).

20

Inheritance (Romans 4:13)

We come to a slightly new viewpoint within the argument of Romans 3:21–4:25. So far the apostle has focused on justification. Justification deals with the beginning of the Christian life. No one is a child of God until he or she is justified before God. Up to this point this had been Paul's concern. He has mentioned how we first receive righteousness (3:21), how we are justified (3:24,28) and how Abraham was justified (4:3, quoting Gen. 15:6). In the life of Abraham this is first stated in Genesis 15:6 although it took place even earlier. For there was faith as early as the events of Genesis 12:1–3 or perhaps even within the events of Genesis 11:26–32.

Now there is a new turn of thought as Paul introduces the idea of inheritance, 'the promise . . . that he would be heir'. Inheritance is the goal of salvation. We are given a free salvation in order to inherit. When a father has a child, the beginning of the child's existence is life, membership of the family, equal sonship with every other child in the family. The destiny of the child is to inherit the blessings and possessions of the family.

Paul's point in Romans 4:13–16 is to tell us that the way to inherit the blessings of God our heavenly Father is by means of justification by faith only.

   Paul says: *For this promise to Abraham and his seed that he should inherit the world was not through the law but through the righteousness of faith* (Rom. 4:13). We may open up the matter in five major points.

The first major point is that justification and inheritance are distinct.

Initial salvation and inheritance are not the same. Getting to heaven is a sure and certain part of justification (Rom. 5:2) but inheritance *in* glory is not. Justification is by faith only. Inheritance is never a matter only of faith.

   Justification and inheritance are not the same. Abraham was promised many blessings in connection with the land of Canaan and the birth of a 'seed'. Paul's exact topic in Romans 4:13–21 is not exclusively justification but rather how justification leads on to inheriting these promises. Inheritance is not getting to heaven.

   There are several reasons for asserting that justification and inheritance are quite different ideas (although Paul's point is that it is only through justifying faith that we ever get to our inheritance).

Justification is initial salvation; inheritance is the fruit of salvation.

In Romans 4, Paul is commenting upon the story of Abraham, and in that story it is quite clear that justification and inheritance are distinct. Abraham's justification is first mentioned in Genesis 15:6. He was certainly justified at that point. The inheritance is mentioned in the next verses (Gen. 15:7,8). 'I brought you out . . . to give you this land . . . to inherit it,' says God to Abraham. The inheritance is not Abraham's justification, which he already has. Rather it is the land and associated blessings which God wants to give Abraham as a gift; the inheritance is in the future. This is clear enough. Justification and inheritance are different.

Justification and inheritance are distinct in that they are obtained in different ways.

Justification comes with our first faith; inheritance comes by persistent faith. Paul keeps on saying that we are justified initially by faith alone (Rom. 3:22,25,28; 4:3,5, and so on). We have seen this in the case of Abraham (4:1–5) and David (4:6–8). It is not a matter of circumcision or Israelite nationality (4:9–12). It is not a matter of keeping the Mosaic law, which is supremely indicated by obedience to the command concerning circumcision. Nor is heaven obtained by works. That too is by faith alone and is secure for us the moment we believe. Paul makes this clear in Romans 5:1–2. 'Being justified by faith we have peace with God'. Paul can immediately add, 'and we rejoice in the expectation of the glory of God'. The expectation of getting to heaven correlates with justification. If we are justified we are as good as in heaven already. We are seated in the heavenly places. Those whom God has justified he has already glorified in plan and purpose and position (Rom. 8:30).

But inheritance is different. Inheritance comes not by faith alone but by persistence in faith. Whenever inheritance is the theme – anywhere in the New Testament – there is always mention in the surrounding context of persistent faith (as we shall find here in Rom. 4) or of godly character, or there is mention of works of faith rather than works of Mosaic legislation. Simple faith brings justification. Simple faith brings assurance of heaven. But it is persistent faith that brings us to our inheritance.

The crucial timing of justification and inheritance are different

Abraham was already justified by the time mentioned in Genesis 15:6. But he began to inherit at the point mentioned in Genesis 22. In Genesis 22:17, after the oath of Genesis 22:16, Abraham is told that his seed will inherit the territory of his enemies, Canaan. The actual possession of the inheritance is still in the future, but by oath it is already his. His inheritance is given to him by oath as a reward for the obedience of faith. This is quite different from justification.

Justification cannot be lost; inheritance may be lost.

Inheritance is conditional. We shall come to this in due course. In Romans 8 Paul says condemnation is impossible in Christ and that nothing can separate us from the love of Christ. He does not put any 'if' in at that point. But in dealing with inheritance (Rom. 8:17), he says we are 'heirs of God and fellow-heirs with Christ, provided that . . .'. There is no 'provided that' in connection with justification. But justification and inheritance are different.

21

Abraham's Inheritance (Romans 4:13)

Justification relates to the promise of acceptance before God as righteous and to assurance of heaven; but inheritance relates to the promises of ministry and usefulness, experience of God's kingdom, achievement of God's will, honour and reward in heaven.

A second major matter is that justification opens the way to the obtaining of inheritance.

Paul says, 'this promise . . . was . . . through the righteousness of faith'. Our righteous position before God makes it possible for us to press on to fellowship with God. Provided we continue in faith and patience (Heb. 6:12), we shall 'inherit the promises'. This also highlights the fact that justification and inheritance are different. If one is the route to the other, then the two are different. There was an inheritance for Abraham; he got to it by faith without the Mosaic law. The same will be true for us, if we persist in faith. Without being righteous in God's sight with the 'reckoned' righteousness of Jesus we shall never be able to inherit the promises of God. It is through being in a righteous position before God that we are able to enjoy fellowship with him, able to pray to him, able to persist in prayer, able to hold on to God no matter what is happening to us.

The third major matter is that the inheritance is 'the world'.

I have a feeling that the Christian church has yet to explore fully the extent of the inheritance, but we can use the present passage to help us make a start in finding an answer. Paul surprises us by speaking of 'the world', because 'the world' is never mentioned in Genesis. However Paul sees that the many promises to Abraham amount to being given 'the world'. Consider for a moment the promises to Abraham.

1. For Abraham, the inheritance was land. God spoke of 'the land I will show you' (Gen. 12:1).
2. The inheritance involved a nation. God said, 'I will make of you a . . . nation,' (Gen. 12:2).
3. The inheritance included numerical increase, multiplication ('. . . a great nation', Gen. 12:2).
4. The inheritance began with Isaac. Abraham was to have a child from his own loins (Gen. 15:4).
5. The inheritance included personal blessing. 'I will bless you,' said God (Gen. 12:2).
6. The inheritance included an honourable name ('I will make your name great', Gen. 12:2).
7. Abraham was told that he would be a channel of blessing to others ('you will be a blessing', Gen. 12:2).

8. It is also promised that he will be a determining factor in the future story of the kingdom of God. The way in which people relate to Abraham and what God is doing through him determines whether they will be blessed or cursed (Gen. 12:2).

9. The extent of the blessing that will come through Abraham is world-wide and international (Gen. 12:3).

These promises are repeated and expanded in Abraham's story. A keyword is introduced in Genesis 12:7. 'To your seed I will give this land.' The promise of land is repeated; the promise of a child is more explicit.

The promise comes again in Genesis 13:14–17. The land of Israel is defined more precisely ('All this land that you see,' 13:15); so also is the seed ('to you and to your seed', 13:15). Its duration is emphasized ('for ever', 13:15). The sheer quantity of Abraham's seed is also accentuated ('like the dust of the earth').

In Genesis 15:4–5 we reach a point where Abraham is having doubts (15:2–3). God repeats the promise, expanding and clarifying it. The seed will include a son for Abraham, begotten by himself, not adopted (15:4). The magnitude of the seed is also repeated ('count the stars . . . so shall your seed be', 15:5). In Genesis 15:7 God speaks of giving Abraham the land for him 'to inherit it'. The Authorized Version (and NKJ) rightly uses the word 'inherit', for the Hebrew word means 'to get as an inheritance'. 'How can I know that I shall inherit it?' Abraham asks (Gen. 15:8). In a deep sleep the inheritance is further defined. Some future history is outlined (Gen. 15:13). The area of the inheritance is again specified (15:18–21), only it is larger than mentioned before (in 13:15).

In Genesis 17:4–8 the promises are repeated and enlarged and in 17:16,18b,21 the actual time of the birth of Abraham's child is made known. The promise is given again in Genesis 18:10.

In Genesis 22:16–18, after Abraham reaches the pinnacle of obedience, God takes an oath (22:15); the promise has now been ratified. Numerical increase, possession of Canaan, world-wide blessing are all promised in an oath. The oath means that the promise has been obtained. By faith and patience Abraham has inherited the promise. The promise is never given again. It does not have to be. It has been obtained.

Again we can see that Abraham's justification (Gen. 15:6 or maybe earlier) opens up the way for him to inherit the promises of God. Because he was 'reckoned righteous' he was in a position to approach God, to ask questions when he had doubts, to come back to God again when he wandered.

For us too, justification is the foundation of all blessings. When God justifies us we have peace. We are right with God. We know we shall be with him in heaven. When we know that we are clothed with the righteousness of Jesus, we are ready to press on to our inheritance.

22

Abraham's Heirs (Romans 4:13)

The fourth major matter in this verse is that the heirs are 'Abraham and his seed'.

Actually the phrase 'seed of Abraham' has within it a fourfold ambiguity. It can be taken as a singular 'one seed' or as a collective word meaning 'thousands of seeds'. The same word is both singular and collective, a bit like the English word 'sheep' which has the same form whether it is 'one sheep' or 'many sheep'. Fortunately the English words 'seed' or 'offspring' are also able to be used as both singular and collective. For this reason it is useful to use the words 'seed' or 'offspring' in translation. 'Descendant' does not have the same ambiguity. 'Seed' can also be taken in a purely natural way and in a supernatural way.

This leads to four possible ways of taking the word 'seed', all of which have some validity.

1. Naturally and singularly, the 'seed of Abraham' is Isaac.
2. Naturally and collectively, the 'seed of Abraham' is the nation of Israel.
3. Supernaturally and singularly, the 'seed of Abraham' is Jesus (see Gal. 3:16).

4. Supernaturally and collectively, the 'seed of Abraham' is the total number of Christians (see Gal. 3:29).

So 'the seed' is a very comprehensive idea. Abraham was promised something that involved his being given the earth.

1. The promise was passed on to Isaac.
2. It involved the coming into being of the nation of Israel.
3. The promise was fulfilled through Jesus.
4. The promise is inherited by those who are fellow-heirs with Christ.

All of this helps us to see what the inheritance is for the Christian. Paul will take this up in fuller detail in Romans 8:17: 'heirs of God and fellow-heirs with Christ'. The Christian is a child of Abraham. He or she is a fellow-heir with Jesus. Like Abraham he or she will inherit the nations, for the nations will come to Jesus through his people. Like Abraham he or she will be personally blessed as he or she persists in faith and patience. Like Abraham he or she will have a name from God and will receive honour and glory. Like Abraham he or she will have a calling and that calling will involve being a channel of blessing to others. The inheritance is 'for Abraham and his seed'. It began with Abraham. It involved God's using the nation of Israel. It revolves around Jesus who is the heir who will inherit the nations. It involves the church. And then it will involve the nation of Israel again, for 'all Israel will be saved'. These are points that Paul will take up further along in his letter, in Romans 8:17–25 and 11:11–32.

A fifth major point is that the inheritance is not gained through the law.

This is a very striking matter because after the giving of the law the inheritance for Israel was through the law. In the Mosaic law this point is made again and again. Under the law, 'the inheritance' was the land. Enjoyment of inheritance was a matter of obeying the Mosaic law. 'Hear now, O Israel, the decrees and laws . . . so that you may . . . inherit the land' (Deut. 4:1; see also 6:18). The Israelites would lose their inheritance if they were disobedient (Deut. 28:58,63). They could possibly get it back if they could be renewed unto repentance. 'He will bring you back to the land . . . and you will inherit it' (Deut. 30:5). Although most of the people of Judah were exiled to Babylon because of idolatry, God kept their inheritance for them. When they repented of their breach of the covenant of law God brought them back.

This means that there is here in Romans 4:13 a deliberate contrast between the kind of obedience demanded from Abraham and the kind of obedience demanded under the law. The Christian is the seed of Abraham; he or she is not under the law. Abrahamic obedience did not require obedience to the Mosaic institutions, which did not yet exist. Territorial inheritance was attained in Israel by the law. Even if their obedience was external, material, physical, nationalistic, it would bring them blessing at a certain level. The law could, to some extent, (if the tenth commandment were overlooked) be attained by any Israelite, regenerate or unregenerate, who was externally obedient to the Mosaic law.

The obedience that brings the Christian his or her inheritance is analogous but contrasting. The equivalent to the law in the New Testament is the Holy Spirit. The starting point of receiving inheritance is justification but what is required is persistent faith, rather than obedience to the Mosaic law. Romans 4 begins by emphasizing the starting point (justification by faith, 4:1–12), then goes on to deal with how inheritance is attained (by persistent faith, 4:13–21). Subsequently Paul will introduce an 'if' (Rom. 8:17).

The 'reward consisting of inheritance' (Col. 3:24) is open to the person who has been justified by faith. What is needed for the inheritance to be reached is to stand before God, righteous by faith, and then persist in that faith! Then, as happened in the story of Abraham, the promises will be obtained. The person who is justified is 'qualified' or 'authorised' for the inheritance (Col. 1:12). Paul thinks of the inheritance as something that is open to the Christian, but is dependent on persistent faith not upon works of the law.

In Romans 4:13–14 Paul widens the promises of land given to Abraham. Paul is deliberately repudiating the nationalistic and legalistic approach to inheritance within the Mosaic covenant, and pointing to faith alone as the starting point of an ongoing faith which will receive the inheritance. 'The promise' in Romans 4:13 does not concern justification (since it looks to the new heavens and earth) but it comes about through righteousness by faith, that is it is only open to those who are justified by faith. It is in total contrast to the method of inheriting by legalistic obedience.

Paul is dealing with the goal of salvation, the reward that salvation makes possible. It is not reached through law-keeping but is reached through this 'righteousness of faith' that he has referred to.

23

Inheritance and Law (Romans 4:14)

The main assertion of Romans 4:13–17a is that inheriting the promises of God does not come by the law but comes 'through' being justified by faith in the Lord Jesus Christ. Paul has laid this down emphatically. 'This promise . . . was not through the law but through the righteousness of faith.' Now he goes on to explain. He gives several reasons why the inheritance cannot be by the Mosaic law.

The first reason is that pursuing inheritance by law would nullify faith.

He says: *For if those of the law are heirs, faith is emptied and the promise is brought to nothing* (Rom. 4:14).

The phrase 'those of the law' could refer to Jews. If reaching our inheritance requires being under the law, Jewish people have an advantage. They are circumcised and are more under the law than gentiles. The promise about world-wide blessing coming to gentiles would obviously be nullified. If inheritance requires keeping the Mosaic law gentiles could only get inheritance by becoming Jews first.

Paul has not yet brought into consideration the tenth commandment. He will do so in Romans 7. If 'those of the law' takes into account the tenth commandment, inheritance is altogether impossible. For no one has ever freed his or her heart from covetousness towards sin simply by means of the tenth commandment. Paul will tell us that it intensifies defeat under the regime of sin.

But Paul's point is more practical than any of this. For Paul 'the law is not of faith' (as he put it in Galatians). It does not require faith to be under the law.

Consider the story of Abraham again. In Genesis 12:1–9 he believes God when a call comes to him to leave home and family. No legislation was involved in this, but it required faith. He had to trust God and leave home not knowing precisely where he would be going. But when you are under law you do know where you are going. It is all very clearly laid down in writing. 'You shall . . . you shall not . . . '. No faith is required.

Consider Genesis 12:10–20. There was a famine and Abraham was so alarmed he left the place he was called to and went to Egypt. There was no law against his doing so, but it was a lapse of faith.

Consider Genesis 13:1–18. There was a dispute about land (13:6) between Abraham and Lot. Abraham magnanimously let Lot have the best of the land. He was not following any law, but he was trusting in God to keep him safe after an impoverishing decision.

Consider Genesis 14:1–24. There was nothing in the Mosaic law (yet to be written) that demanded Abraham go out in battle against neighbouring kings to rescue his nephew Lot. Lot had just been ungenerous to his uncle, and the Mosaic law would not have demanded that Abraham show such great kindness in rescuing Lot despite his greed and his worldliness. But it required faith.

At the end of the battle Abraham was weary. He had turned down the offer of gain from the king of Sodom, He was trusting in the praying of a great priest of God, Melchizedek. God came to him: 'I am your shield' (exactly what Abraham needed after a fierce battle) 'and your exceedingly great reward' (exactly what Abraham needed after turning down reward from the king of Sodom). This is what the godly life is like. Law-keeping does not come into this story of Abraham. He was moving towards inher-iting the promises by persistent faith in God no matter what happened to him.

And so we could go on right the way through the story of Abraham. Getting to the inheritance did not involve Abraham in law-keeping but it involved him in faith. He had to trust God against great delays, against his own great weakness.

Or consider the greatest test of faith of all: the offering up of Isaac. We read that God tested Abraham (Gen. 22:1). He was not testing Abraham's obedience to the Mosaic law or anything like it. It was a great test of Abraham's faith, of his willingness to suffer, of his willingness to see all of his hopes dashed to nothing. He had to believe that God was able to raise Isaac from the dead if necessary. What bought the inheritance to Abraham was rising to a great height of faith. We remember what happened. In sheer faith Abraham did precisely what God asked. It was great obedience, but it was not obedience to a law code, it was obedience to the personal requirements of God directly laid upon him. It was obedience that required immense faith. But Abraham obeyed, and received the promises! It was his faith that had brought the oath of God into his life (Gen. 22:16).

God's design is that we get to our inheritance by persistent faith. If the inheritance came simply by law-keeping the entire matter of clinging to the promises of God in persistent faith would be pushed aside. If those of the law are heirs — whether by being Jews or whether by being gentiles who have put themselves under the law — the life of faith is turned aside into a different kind of life altogether. Living on the promises would become a matter of living on the law. The promise would be nullified. It would be for Jews, for Judaized gentiles, for people who kept the written law code, for those who were highly moral in theory but who showed little love in practice and for those who could never keep the tenth commandment. It would abort God's entire wish that his people show trust in his ability to keep his promises. The great challenges of living by faith go far beyond anything mentioned in the Mosaic law or any other codified law. Abraham is the model and in his day the law did not even exist. Yet by faith he reached great heights of obedience. It is by faith and patience that one inherits the promises and in no other way.

The Law Works Wrath (Romans 4:15)

The second reason why inheritance cannot be by the law is that in any relationship to God and among God's people law rouses anger.

For the law works wrath, and where there is no law there is no transgression (Rom. 4:15).

Paul is arguing that inheritance is received by faith (4:13) and that the law is not a matter of faith but rather annuls faith (4:14). It damages our relationship with God and his people; it does not help such a relationship at all. In its deepest meaning the law is always broken. Even when taken purely externally it is often broken, although it is possible to keep the law at a superficial level. The law does not arouse love of God or spur us on to liveliness in joy or give motivation that excites us to live for God and his will. On the contrary it 'works wrath'.

It can only arouse God's wrath.

If our relationship to God has law interposed between us and him, it can only arouse his anger. We cannot keep his law perfectly. The law can only pinpoint our sins and arouse God's hostility if he views us in such a way.

The law can only arouse our wrath against God.

When we try to relate to God via law-keeping and resolu- tions and vows and the rules and regulations of what we are promising to do, we fail again and again and then we find ourselves getting full of resentment. It is not only rousing God's wrath against us; it is rousing our wrath against him.

The law rouses wrath and resentment in human relationships.

The church of Galatia was, it seems, the most law-centred of all of Paul's churches. But it was to that very church that he had to write, 'If you keep biting and devouring one another, watch out or you will be destroyed by each other' (Gal. 5:15). Where Christians or friends or married couples relate to each other by way of laws, recriminations break out. Accusations of failure, charges that the 'law has been broken' multiply. Where there is plenty of law there is plenty of broken law, plenty of material for accusation, plenty of Pharisaism, plenty of recriminations.

The law rouses wrath and resentment towards ourselves.

We become disgusted with our own failures. 'O wretched man that I am' is our cry. Soon we despise ourselves. We are not truly convicted of sin. We are convicted of our righteousness. We ought to be keeping this law! Why do I not keep this standard? The good that I would I do not, we say to ourselves. If we live this way we eventually lose self-respect. We begin to regard ourselves as worthless. We regard ourselves as junk, because we feel so condemned. 'The law works wrath' in countless ways!

For where there is no law there is no transgression. The reason why the law does such damage in our relation to God, our relation to others, our relation to ourselves, is that God's law or any other codified law only throws up in our face the fact of sin. It makes sin worse. It turns sin into 'transgression' which is 'sin explicit', 'sin defined', 'sin made into a breach of a rule'. Where there is no law sin is there but it is not thrown into our face.

When the law is dealt with (a theme that Paul will get to in Romans 7) wrath is turned aside. Where there is no law God's wrath is turned aside. There is no condemnation towards us coming from God. We are free to follow him in faith and in love. When we fall we get up. Where there is no law there is freedom from guilt and our hearts are free to rise in love to God.

Where there is no law, human relationships experience graciousness. Husbands and wives cease to practise condemnation and complaining criticisms.

Where there is no law, our hearts are not burdened with shame. When we know that God is not relating to us in such a 'Mosaic' way, we feel confident in his presence.

It does not mean that we run riot into sinful ways. God has a will for our lives. Freedom from law is not freedom from obedience or freedom from righteousness. But it is freedom from a certain manner of seeking to get to righteousness.

But how can there ever be 'no law'? Paul has already told us. We are justified 'as a gift, by his grace, through the redemption that is in Christ Jesus. God put him forward as a sacrifice to turn away anger, through faith and by means of blood' (Rom. 3:24,25). Later he will go even further. Paul's main point in Romans 7 will be to tell us that we should not try to live under the Mosaic law. We have actually 'died' to it, in order to be fruitful towards God.

The way for us to get to our inheritance is 'through the righteousness of faith'. We believe in God's promises and we believe again. When we fall we go on believing. When we are facing opposition we go on believing. When we feel as good as dead we go on believing. Faith works its way through to godliness, to patience, to endurance, to content-ment. Faith works its way through to love. We do not allow ourselves to be condemned by the law. We do not con-demn anyone else by the law either. We go on and on trusting the promises of God. We dare to believe we are free from condemnation. We venture to release our enemies to God and God alone. When we stray from God's will we believe we can still get back and be used by God again. Whatever comes our way we go on believing. Faith will lead us into heights of godliness, as it led Abraham into heights of godliness. When we fall we grieve our Father but we still do not come under condemnation. We go on believing no matter what, and in that way we inherit the promises.

25

Grace and Faith (Romans 4:16)

The third reason why inheritance cannot be by the law is that attempting to relate to God by law makes inheritance uncertain, but faith makes it certain for all believers.

Paul says: *For this reason*, that is, because law excludes faith and rouses wrath, *the promise is by faith in order that it may be according to grace, in order that the promise might be sure to all the seed, not only to those who are of the law but also to those who are of the faith of Abraham. He is the father of us all* (Rom. 4:16).

We must notice first of all that Paul is not talking of justification or initial salvation. He does not say, 'the promise of justification is by faith in order that it may be according to grace, so that the promise of justification is sure . . . '. Rather he says, 'the promise of inheritance is by faith in order that it may be according to grace, in order that the promise might be sure . . . '. We notice also that Paul does not say, 'so that the promise is sure' (which is what he could have said if he had been referring to justification). Rather he says, 'in order that the promise might be sure . . . '. Romans 8:17 ('if') makes it clear that the promise of inheritance is not automatically sure, but it might be sure by being pursued by faith and by God's grace. Abraham was already justified. The promise concerned the remainder of his life and what God wanted to give him as an inheritance.

We can develop these two points. The promise was that the seed of Abraham, Jesus and all of his people, should 'inherit the earth' (Matt. 5:5). But how certain can we be that we shall attain the inheritance?

The law is full of uncertainty.

If the inheritance were by law it would undoubtedly be unreliable in the case of gentiles. The law was not designed for gentiles. To pursue the inheritance by the Mosaic law would mean that gentiles would have to abandon their culture and become Jews. The promise is by faith in order that it might be sure to *all* the seed, not only to those who are of the law but also to those who are of the faith of Abraham. He is the father of us *all*.

But apart from the nationalistic aspect of the matter, to pursue the inheritance by law would make it very uncertain because the deepest aspects of the law cannot be kept. Who can claim they have kept the tenth commandment and not even had the slightest desire for sin?

If the tenth commandment is left out of consideration and the law is viewed more superficially, then such obedience does not lead to great spirituality. God is looking for high obedience for the inheritance to be given. It was only after persistent and obedient faith that God said to Abraham,

'Now I know that you fear me' and the inheritance was securely obtained. The law of Moses could never have brought Abraham to such a high level of obedience and trust. It takes more than not stealing, not lying, not committing adultery, and so on. Whichever way it is approached, to seek inheritance by law-keeping makes the possibility of attaining it very uncertain.

It is faith and grace which make the inheritance sure.

On God's side there is grace. He wants to graciously enable us and protect us and provide for us. In Genesis 15:8 Abraham expresses anxiety: 'how can I know that I will gain possession of it?' (15:8). It is uncertainty concerning a future inheritance. In response God gives his covenant. The inheritance is both given and taken. No obstacles, no delays, no weakness in ourselves will prevent it from coming to us. On our side what is required is faith. If God is gracious and if we are believing the inheritance is sure: nothing can stop it. God wants us to go on believing. God wants to go on ministering grace.

Provided we continue in faith God will bring us through all kinds of obstacles.

The inheritance is not made sure by law, or by will-power, or by our ability or cleverness. It is made sure by God's grace, flowing down to us through our persisting in faith.

'God . . . has caused us to be born again . . . in order that we may obtain an inheritance, . . . reserved in heaven for you who by the power of God are being guarded through faith . . . ' (1 Pet. 1:3,4). 'By the power of God . . . through faith.' The inheritance is made sure on God's side by his grace and power, on our side by faith.

What will finally secure the inheritance is when God takes an oath. In Genesis 15:8 Abraham expressed anxiety about the certainty of the inheritance. God offered him a covenant, but no oath of the covenant was given. The covenant was on offer but it had not yet been ratified. In Genesis 22:16 the oath was given and the inheritance was sure and certain. What had made the inheritance sure and certain was not law but grace and faith.

God's inheritance is fixed once an oath has been taken.

David experienced a covenant oath at the time mentioned in 2 Samuel 7. From that point on the inheritance of David (that Jesus would come in his line) was fixed. Not even his sin with Bathsheba could abort it. Psalm 89 is the inspired commentary on the matter (note Ps. 89:1–4, 29–37). Through faith the inheritance is shielded by God's power. Grace and assurance go together. The inheritance is safe while we believe. It is not sure absolutely, before the oath is taken. Saul lost his inheritance, as did the Israelites in the wilderness. But inheritance is sure while we believe. When it is 'obtained' by God's oath then it is sure beyond the possibility of loss.

It is sure in this way for all the seed. Faith and grace lead to equal opportunity for Jew and gentile. All the seed may surely and certainly experience God's oath and lay up a never-failing inheritance, provided they continue to live on God's grace, that is, continue to live by faith. Faith and grace go together.

26

Faith (Romans 4:16)

Paul says, 'the promise is by faith . . . ' (Rom. 4:16). God's promised inheritance comes by faith.

Faith is the greatest secret of the Christian life. The Christian life begins with faith and ends with love. The whole Christian life is a life of faith (2 Cor. 5:7). Christians are the 'household of faith' (Gal. 6:10). The Christian life begins with faith (Eph. 2:8) and goes on by faith (Rom. 14:1,2,23; 2 Pet. 1:5; 1 Thes. 3:10). By faith we are heir to all of the promises of God (Gal. 3:7–9). The New Testament speaks of 'precious' faith (2 Pet. 1:1). It is the starting point of all blessings. Every gift is to be received by faith. All the promises are 'yes' in Jesus, but we have to say the 'Amen'. (2 Cor. 1). God works and gives promises and God calls us, but we must believe. In the matter of faith we are thinking of what happens in us.

We must think a little about what it means to have faith. Let us think first about what faith is not.

1. Faith is not blind hopefulness. It is not credulity or gullibility. It is not a 'leap in the dark' but a leap into the light! It is based on the reliability of God's Word (Tit. 1:2). God does not lie (2 Sam. 7:28).
2. Faith is not anything natural. It is not the same as 'faith to get on a bus' (which is not faith but a feeling that

probably all will be well). The Bible says, 'Not all people have faith' (2 Thes. 3:2).

3. Faith is not thoughtless optimism. This is the characteristic of the foolish man (think of Matt. 7:24–27).

4. Faith is not intellectual understanding only. It is not understanding doctrine. It is not even believing that the doctrine is true.

5. Faith is not agreeing with the teaching of the church. It is not agreeing with what you don't understand. All Christians (not just ministers) are meant to understand the Word of God. 'They will all be taught of God' (John. 6:45).

6. Faith is not persuading ourselves when we are not really convinced. Certain types of healing meeting try to work up faith. But often they are trying to get us to persuade ourselves against what we believe in our hearts. This kind of self-persuasion is not faith at all. There is no strain or struggle in faith. Abraham did not waver in his confidence in the promise of God. He was persuaded that the one who promised was able also to perform. He was not struggling or pretending or making claims he did not really feel in his heart.

What then does it mean to have faith?

1. Faith is believing God. It is taking him at his word. It is taking seriously what he says.

2. Faith is looking for God to give us what we are sure he is offering. It is putting out our hand to take what we know he offers. It is looking to him because we know he is there to fulfil his promises. It is feeding on him

because we know he is bread for our souls. It is drinking from him because we know he promises to quench the thirst of our souls. It is running into his strong tower. It is confidence in God because he has spoken to us.

We trust in God to be our Father. We hold on to the faithfulness of God (Mark. 11:22). We trust in Jesus to be our Saviour in a thousand crises and difficulties and burdens. We live by the faithfulness of the Son of God. We believe in his name (John. 1:12; Acts 3:16), his Lordship (Rom. 10:9–10; Acts 9:42; 11:17; 22:19). We trust him to be the light, the way, the truth, the resurrection and the life.

We believe in the Word of God, the Scriptures (Luke 24:25; 2 Thes. 1:10; John 2:22; 5:46,47; Acts 24:14). We believe in God's promises (Rom. 4:20; Luke. 1:45; 8:12; 1 John 5:10).

We do not have faith in ourselves except to the extent that we know that God is with us. We do not trust ourselves, our wisdom, our feelings. We do not trust false teachers. We do not put our confidence in people. It is better to trust in the Lord than to put confidence in princes.

Justifying faith has to become inheriting faith. It is the same faith but it has to be applied to new situations. The faith that saved us when we trusted God's first promise has to keep us when we trust his later promises.

Saving faith has to become diligent faith, continuing faith. We have to hold fast to the confidence that we had at first. Faith starts by trusting Jesus alone. It does not look at all to itself. We are saved without works. But then saving faith must become diligent faith. It begins by doing nothing and receiving everything. Then it starts to live for God. It becomes active faith, working faith, obeying faith. It does things for God. It perseveres. Faith goes through testings, obstacles, delays, temptations. By faith alone we are justified. By faith and patience we inherit the promises (Heb. 6:12). Our saving faith is preserved by Jesus, but on the human side, we must apply our faith, we must continue in faith.

Faith first of all saves us by linking us to Jesus. Strictly speaking it is not faith that saves, it is Jesus who saves. Faith is simply the way we latch on to Jesus. Then faith links us to the power of God (Rom. 1:16; Eph. 1:19; 1 Thes. 2:13). It gives us eternal life (1 Tim. 1:16; John 3:15,16; 5:24; 6:40,47; 20:31; 1 John 5:13). It unites us to Christ (Acts 5:14), gives blessing (Luke 1:45) and the benefits of Christ's death (Rom. 3:25). It prevents us from abiding in darkness (John 11:46). It makes the Word effective (Heb. 4:2,3). It sees the glory of God (John 11:40).

Paul says, 'For this reason the promise is by faith . . .' God's promised inheritance is never going to come by the law. It comes by our trusting in God, no matter what. By faith and patience we inherit the promises.

27

How Faith Works (Romans 4:16–17)

To relate to God by law makes inheritance uncertain, but faith makes it certain for all believers. Paul says: *For this reason the promise is by faith in order that . . . the promise might be sure to all the seed, not only to those who are of the law but also to those who are of the faith of Abraham. He is the father of us all* (Rom. 4:16), *as it is written, 'I have appointed you a father of many nations'* (Rom. 4:17a).

Inheritance must be pursued by faith, or (to put the same thing another way) by persistently trusting in God's grace. Then we shall 'inherit the promises'. We shall enter into the great joy of serving God, of experiencing personal blessing, of having a calling, of finding enablement, of bringing about numerical increase of 'Abraham's seed', of getting an honourable name, of being a channel of blessing, of experiencing the kingdom, of reaching nations, of laying up treasure in heaven, of experiencing a high level of glory in the new heavens and new earth. All will come to us surely and certainly if pursued by faith and by trusting in God's grace.

This rich blessing is open to all of the people of Jesus, all who are the seed of Abraham because they are in Christ who is the seed of Abraham. The promise is 'sure to all the seed'. Here the phrase 'those who are of the law' refers to

Jewish Christians; before (4:14) it referred to unsaved Jews and those like them who sought inheritance by legalism.

There is only one people of God. Jewish believers and gentile believers are in the one church on an entirely equal footing. Abraham is not the father of the Jewish subsection of the church, or the gentile subsection of the church. He is the father of us all. This was the point of Genesis 17:5 which Paul quotes: 'as it is written, "I have appointed you a father of many nations".'

At this point Paul inconspicuously glides into a new part of the argument. The Greek is complicated and may be translated: 'He is the father of us all, as it is written, "I have appointed you a father of many nations", before the one he believed. . . .' The phrase 'before the one he believed' starts a new line of thought taking its beginning from the ideas of the previous phrases. A good way to bring out Paul's thought is to repeat 'He is the father of many nations.' I translate as follows.

For this reason, the promise is by faith in order that it may be according to grace, in order that the promise might be sure to all the seed, not only to those who are of the law but also to those who are of the faith of Abraham. He is the father of us all (Rom. 4:16), *as it is written, 'I have appointed you a father of many nations'* (Rom. 4:17a). *Abraham is the father of many nations in the presence of the one he believed, God, who gives life to the dead and calls things that have no existence so that they come into existence* (Rom. 4:17b).

In Romans 4:17b Paul begins to describe this faith that is justifying faith (4:1–12) but is also inheriting faith (4:13–21). Romans 4:22–25 will make the point that it is the same faith in both situations. Faith begun brings justification; faith continued brings inheritance. Romans 4:17b–21 now puts before us a wonderful description of how faith works when it is persevering and laying hold of the promises of God despite great opposition and conflict. There are a number of aspects of inheriting faith which we must notice.

Faith takes notice of what is promised 'in the presence of God'.

Paul says, 'Abraham is the father of many nations in the presence of the one he believed, God, who gives life to the dead. . . .' God had a programme in mind. He planned to make Abraham the father of many nations. Whole nations of the world would turn to Jesus and so become 'children of Abraham'. This was not yet true in actuality. It was not yet a matter of history. Abraham as the father of many nations existed only in the mind of God. But when Abraham was before God he regarded himself as what God promised he would be. Faith sees what God sees and reveals what will actually be the case one day. It had not happened yet but that was the way Abraham saw things. 'Abraham is the father of many nations in the presence of the one he believed.' This is the way faith works. It sees things the way they will be, not the way they are. Faith is a conviction about things not seen (Heb. 11:1). We do not yet see with the physical eye every knee bowing to Jesus. We do not literally see every tongue confessing that Jesus Christ is Lord. But faith sees it anyway. Faith says, 'When I am in the presence of God I see the way it will be. I see every knee bowed; I hear every tongue confessing. This is the way I see it, before God.'

Faith has to relate to God's word.

Abraham was able to exercise faith because God had spoken. God had said to him: 'I have appointed you a father of many nations.' When Abraham was before God he saw himself as the father of many nations because that is what God had said about him.

This is a very important matter. Many strange 'faith teachings' go astray because they do not see that faith always relates to what God has said. Faith is believing God. It is taking God at his word. If he has not given a word about any particular matter it is not possible to exercise faith. The essence of faith is to be able to say: 'I believe God, that it shall be just as it has been spoken to me' (Acts 27:25). If it has not been spoken it cannot be believed. When Abraham believed God for his inheritance it was because God had spoken to him.

28

Believing God (Romans 4:17)

In Romans 4:17–21 Paul is elaborating what he wants to say about faith. Our entire position in the kingdom of God depends on faith. 'Faith' is mentioned again and again in these verses (Rom. 3:22,25,26,27,28,30,31; 4:3,5,9,11,12, 13,16).

When we first believe we are covered with the right-eousness of Jesus. Then faith also enables the Christian to get to his or her inheritance. Inheritance is not the same as what I call initial salvation. Initial salvation is forgiveness and justification and new birth and adoption as God's children. Inheritance is what we are saved for. It is where God is taking us. It is what God wants to give us. Inheritance is our reaping the blessings of living for God, and our final salvation which is a matter of reward.

Inheritance comes through our being justified by faith. The Christian life begins with faith and it goes on with faith. Initially salvation is by faith alone; then the inheriting of the rewards and encouragements of God comes by persist-ing in this faith. It is a matter of continuing in the way that we began.

Abraham is the father of us all, says Paul in Romans 4:16. God had spoken to Abraham: 'I have appointed you a father of many nations.' Paul is describing Abraham's faith, showing how it laid hold of God's promises and inherited them. 'Abraham is the father of many nations in the presence of the one he believed, God, who gives life to the dead and calls things that have no existence so that they have an existence' (Rom. 4:17b).

In order to be secure, the inheritance has to come by grace and through faith. Then it can come even to gentiles who do not have the law of Moses. Abraham is the father of all believers, not just Jewish believers (4:16). The Scripture referred to 'many' nations, not just one nation (4:17a).

Abraham's inheritance was the new heavens and new earth foreshadowed in the land of Israel. His inheritance was the coming into being of all believers, foreshadowed in the nation of Israel. His inheritance was Jesus, foreshadowed in the person of Isaac.

Our inheritance is to share in God's plan for Abraham. It is to be the children of Abraham and take our part in this purpose of God to bring in the new heavens and a new earth in which dwells righteousness.

In this life our inheritance is ministry, enablement, impact upon people, contribution to the kingdom of God, exaltation to honour, authority (Acts 19:15), joy (Heb. 1:9), a realm in which we have authority, companionship of Jesus (Heb. 3:14), it is enjoying everything in God's world through Jesus!

There are stages to our inheritance. Mark 10:29–30 says it comes 'in the present age and in the world to come . . . '. In this life it is experiencing God, experiencing the kingdom, fruitfulness, enjoying God's world even now (Matt. 5:3; 1 Cor. 3:20,21; 1 Tim. 4:3–5; Rom. 14:22b says, 'Blessed are those who have no reason to condemn themselves . . . ').

The inheritance is also a matter of enjoying God's world to come. We shall have new bodies, and shall live in a resurrected universe. It is not fully revealed (1 John 3:3) but there will be the new heavens and a new earth in which righteousness dwells. There will be different levels of glory according to the way we have lived in this world. One star differs from another star in glory; so it will be in the resurrection from the dead (1 Cor. 15:41,42).

We reach our inheritance not through the law but through the righteousness that comes by faith. We are first saved by faith only, then we persist in faith. We 'eat his flesh' and 'drink his blood' (John 6:56). That is to say, we live on him as the one who died for us and is alive for us. We remain in him and he remains in us. We abide in him like a branch abides in a tree (see John 15:4–7). When we do that we are able to ask God for anything we need to do his will. By faith we obey his commandments and abide in his love (John 15:9,10). We live 'in' him (1 John 2:6,28). In the same way that we received Jesus at first, so we live in him now (Col. 2:6,7). The Mosaic law does not come into the matter. We receive the Spirit not by law but by the hearing of faith. In this way 'the blessings of Abraham' become ours (Gal. 3:1–14). Legalism and faith are opposites. If you live by rules you are not living by faith. We can have disciplines for ourselves, but they are not rules from God. Faith is the key to every blessing. In Christ neither circumcision nor uncircumcision has any value, but only faith expressing itself in love (Gal. 5:6).

Romans 4:17b–21 is a wonderful description of how this faith works. The sentence is difficult to follow. The Revised English Bible translates it like this: 'In the presence of God, the God who makes the dead live and calls into being things that are not, Abraham had faith.' Or I could paraphrase it: 'In the presence of God who had given him this promise, Abraham had faith. He believed in God as the one who brings the dead to life, and as the one who calls into being things that at present do not exist.'

We are learning lessons about faith, and have seen that faith sees things the way they are in the presence of God. Also, faith has to relate to God's word. Faith is exercised in the presence of God, and in the presence of his Word. Faith is standing on the promises of God. You cannot have faith unless you have a word to stand on. There are two ways in which God's word may come to us. It may come by the general promises that God gives and that are recorded in God's written word. Or God's word may come to us through a special word of revelation. God may give us a promise through the Holy Spirit.

29

Standing on the Promises
(Romans 4:17b–18)

God has given general promises to all his people. 'Seek first God's kingdom and his righteousness, and all these things shall be added to you' (Matt. 6:33). It is true for every Christian. It is true in every situation. As long as we seek first God's kingdom and righteousness we can be sure our needs will be met.

'Upon this rock I will build my church' (Matt. 16:18). It is an absolute promise. There are no conditions at all. Jesus promises he will build his church.

'My God will meet all of your needs,' Paul said to his friends at Philippi (Phil. 4:19). It is a promise that can be taken by any Christian.

'If any of you lack wisdom, he should ask God . . . and it shall be given him' (James 1:5).

Promises like this do not need any further revelations from God. We do not need a special dream or prophecy to tell us that God will meet our needs as we seek his kingdom. The promise has already been given. But there is a second way in which God can give us a promise. A revelation can come to us by the Holy Spirit. God told Abraham about the seed that was to come into existence. Abraham had no Bible. It was a direct revelation to Abraham's heart through the Holy Spirit. God spoke to Abraham. 'I have made you a father of many nations,' God said (Gen. 17:5). In the mind of God it was as good as done. In the presence of God it was already accomplished. By the Holy Spirit Abraham knew about this promise of God. Later God gave a very definite commitment even about the time of Isaac's birth: 'I will return to you about this time next year, and Sarah your wife will have a son' (Gen. 18:10). Again Abraham was not reading any Scripture. He certainly was not meditating on the Mosaic law.

We need to be careful about this. Many people have thought God was speaking to them but have made bad mistakes. Yet the Bible tells us to 'test the spirits' (1 John 4:1) and there would be no point in our being told to test the spirits if there was nothing to test. Some people never have to test the spirits because the Holy Spirit apparently does not speak to them anyway. They have nothing to test! God can still speak by the Holy Spirit. God told Paul at the time of his conversion that he would be an apostle to the gentiles (Acts 26:16–18). When he was in danger of his life travelling by sea to Rome God spoke to him. 'Last night an angel of the God whom I serve stood by me and said "Don't be afraid, Paul. You must stand trial before Caesar; and God has graciously given you the lives of all who sail with you" ' (Acts 27:23,24). So Paul's faith was directed to this special revelation that he had received. 'I have faith in God that it will happen just as he told me' (Acts 27:25). These revelations have to be tested.

A lot of needless suffering comes into the lives of Christians when they try to 'take by faith' something God is not giving. If you do not have a word from God, either as a general promise or as a revelation from the Holy Spirit, you may not be able to 'take by faith' the thing that you want. I would rather people believe too much than believe too little, but confusion and disillusionment comes to Christians when people want to 'claim by faith' blessings concerning which God has not given a word.

What enabled Abraham to battle against many odds was that God had said to him, 'I have appointed you a father of many nations'. God has said to him, 'next year . . . your wife will have a son'. *Against hope but in hope Abraham believed in order that he would become a father of many nations, according to what had been spoken, 'So shall your seed be'* (Rom. 4:18). This is the point: 'Abraham believed . . . according to what had been spoken!' We have seen then two characteristics of faith: faith sees things the way they are in the presence of God, and faith has to relate to God's word. We now move on to the third matter.

Faith holds on to God's ability to resurrect.

Abraham believed God, 'who gives life to the dead . . . ' (Rom. 4:17b). Faith believes in resurrection. God raised Jesus from the dead but God can raise anything and anyone anywhere from the dead. Faith believes in resurrection, not simply in the matter of the resurrection of Jesus (although that was the greatest resurrection of all time), but in God's ability to raise anything and anyone from the dead. Abraham knew that 'his body was as good as dead' (Rom.

4:19) but that did not stop him believing. He knew that God could raise the dead. God asked Abraham on one occasion to put Isaac to death. Even that did not stop him believing. 'Abraham reasoned that God could raise the dead!' (Heb. 11:19).

This is the very essence of faith. We believe in resurrections. When God feels like it he can raise the dead. Paul on one occasion went through great sufferings. He said that he had in his heart the feeling that he was about to die. 'We had in our hearts the sentence of death' (2 Cor. 1:9). But, says Paul, this happens that we might not rely on ourselves but on God who raises the dead (2 Cor. 1:9). God raised Abraham's dead body and Sarah's dead body that Isaac might be born. When we were dead in trespasses and sin (Eph. 2:1), God made us alive (Eph. 2:4). When Paul despaired of life it made him look to one who raises the dead. In a thousand situations Jesus is 'the resurrection and the life'. Faith believes in God who raises the dead.

30

Faith in the Creator (Romans 4:17b–18)

Romans 4:17b–21 is one of the most detailed descriptions of the working of faith that we have in the Bible.

Another characteristic of faith is that faith holds on to God's ability as creator.

Abraham believed God, 'who gives life to the dead, and calls things that have no existence so that they come into existence' (Rom. 4:17b). When God has given you a promise but you are in a situation of difficulty, the problem may be that something has died or that something you need does not exist. In Abraham's case, his body was as good as dead, and the possibility of conceiving a child through the elderly Sarah did not exist. And yet God had given a promise of world-wide blessing coming through the birth of a child.

In our own smaller way we may find ourselves in a similar situation. Is there something in your life that has died? Liveliness? Prayerfulness? Testimony? Power? Love? Expectation? Sensitivity to people? Or is there something you believe God has promised but as yet it does not exist?

Abraham went on believing. He showed he had the kind of faith that would believe in the resurrection of Jesus. Also, his faith looked to God the Creator. He trusted '. . . the God who gives life to the dead and calls things that have no existence so that they come into existence'.

Creation does not have to use pre-existing material.

God had promised Abraham land and a vast number of children. Whole nations, God had said, would be his children. Yet at the moment he did not seem to be able to have one child. But Abraham believed in 'the God who . . . calls things that have no existence so that they come into existence'. He still believed despite the fact that God did not seem to have anything to work on in the case of him and Sarah.

Creation is deeply mysterious.

No one can visualize what takes place when God creates. So in the case of Abraham, he must have been baffled how the promise of God could possibly come to pass. But he did not need to understand. He simply reckoned God could call things that have no existence so that they come into existence.

Creation is speedy.

How long does it take to create? When God gives a promise there may be delay for a long time, but when God decides

to move, how long does it take a Creator to bring something new into being? No time at all!

God's creating takes place by 'calling'.

God created by speaking. He 'calls' things that have no
existence so that they come into existence. Abraham believed this. He reckoned that a mere word from God would
call everything into being that he had been promised.

Conversion is like this. It is creating something out of
nothing (Eph. 2:1–10; 1 Cor. 1:27–29). God can create
something that was not there before. The one thing you
need to exercise faith is a word from God. If you have a
word from God you insist on believing in 'the God who
. . . calls things that have no existence so that they come
into existence'.

A further characteristic of faith is that faith
can face hopelessness when it has a word
from God.

Abraham was in a situation that seemed hopeless. How
could such an elderly man and such a elderly woman expect
a multitude of children? They had never been able to have
even one child despite the decades that they had been
together. But Paul says, 'Against hope but in hope Abraham
believed in order that he would become a father of many
nations, according to what had been spoken, "So shall your

seed be"' (Rom. 4:18). Faith may have to face immense difficulties. There are three of them that are commonplace in the Christian life, one from God, one from Satan and one in ourselves. God may allow great delay. God gave a promise of a child but Abraham had to wait many years before the seed was secured. As well as God's delay we may find that Satan sends opposition. In ourselves we find great weakness. In Abraham's case his body was as good as dead. These are things that constitute an obstacle to faith: God's delay, the devil's opposition, our own weakness.

But Abraham persisted: 'Against hope but in hope Abraham believed . . .'. Faith expects the future to turn out as God said. Everything seemed against Abraham. Humanly speaking there did not seem to be any chance that God's promise would come to pass. Yet he believed 'in hope'. He was confident that the child would come and that he would indeed be the father of many nations.

What enabled him to believe in such a difficult situation? It was the fact that he was clear that God had spoken. 'Abraham believed . . . according to what had been spoken, "So shall your seed be".' He had a definite promise from God and that was enough for him. If God has spoken to us and given us a promise about something yet to come, that word will enable us to hold on despite the, apparently, very difficult situations that stand against us.

We have to be sure that we do indeed have a word from God. We must not try to convince ourselves that God has spoken to us when he has not in fact done so. We have especially to be careful of foolhardiness when it comes to promises of money or predictions of a very successful and

famous future or convictions about a member of the opposite sex. In such areas we can give ourselves promises when
God is not giving them to us. Of course God can give
promises about such things. I am simply saying we have to
be careful.

But when God has given us a clear word, we hold to
what he has said. He can raise the dead. He can bring
something out of nothing. Everything might be against us.
Yet if God has spoken, then his word is faithful. We can
confidently trust him to bring about what he has said.

31

Faith Faces Facts (Romans 4:19–20)

We are looking at the characteristics of faith. We have seen that: faith lives and flourishes 'in the presence of God'; faith has to relate to God's word; faith holds on to God's ability to raise the dead; faith holds on to God's ability as creator; and faith can be optimistic in a situation of hopelessness, because it has a word from God. Now we come to another aspect of faith.

Faith is realistic: it is not afraid to face facts.

Paul goes on to say *And without becoming weak in faith he considered his own body, already as good as dead because he was about a hundred years old, and he considered the deadness of Sarah's womb* (Rom. 4:19). The King James or Authorized Version of 1611 reads, 'he considered *not* his own body'. This is a mistake. The KJV translators of 1611 were using only a few manuscripts and they were not of good quality. Modern published Greek New Testaments make use of about five thousand manuscripts, some of which are more reliable than those used by the KJV.

Most modern translations follow the best manuscripts and say something like: 'without becoming weak in faith

he considered his own body'. Faith is not pretending. It is
not shutting one's eyes to the facts. Faith does not close its
mind and pretend things are other than the way they are.
No, faith takes a good look at the way things are, and then
it says, 'But God has told me that he will do this and that.
I see the way it is but I believe the situation is going to
change because God has told me something about it.' Faith
is not playing a part. It does not have to work itself up or
try to say something it does not really accept as true. There
is no strain in faith. Faith considers the facts but is not
intimidated by them. It is a bold confidence in what God
has said. If God has not spoken, there cannot be faith.

Another aspect of faith is that it is able to overcome doubts.

Paul says, *Yet he did not waver in unbelief with regard to the
promise of God but he was strengthened in faith, by giving glory
to God* (Rom. 4:20).

Abraham faced his weakness. One of the obstacles to faith
in God's promised inheritance is that at times we are almost
overcome by our own weaknesses. And so we say to
ourselves, 'How can God do this for me? How can I really
receive this blessing? I know I am weak in this way and in
that way. Can God really do for me what he has promised?'
We all have weakness! It may be intellectual weakness,
financial weakness, emotional or psychological weakness,
fear of responsibility, vulnerability in one way or another.
Abraham had a physical weakness. He was elderly and there

did not seem to be any hope that someone at his age and with an elderly wife could possibly see a multitude of offspring come into being.

But faith refuses to waver. It refuses unbelief. Abraham was attacked by doubt. Faith can be attacked, but faith is able to triumph over such attacks. Many of us know what it is to be doing that which we feel God has brought us into. Then suddenly – maybe in the middle of the night – we abruptly find the most awful doubts arising. Am I really right? Did God really lead me? This seems too big a venture altogether. Maybe I am not really in the will of God? Abraham was certainly attacked by doubts. In Genesis 15:3 Abraham put his perplexity to the Lord: 'Look, you have not given a seed to me.' Also the incident of Genesis 16:1–4 arose because Abraham was doubting whether he really would have a son through Sarah. But Paul is not referring to being tempted to doubt. He is rather saying that Abraham's faith was able to rise above the attacks on what he was doing. If you believe you are in the will of God but then you become full of doubts, face your doubts. Don't pretend that the facts are other than the way they are. Abraham considered his own body, already as good as dead. He considered the deadness of Sarah's womb. When attacked by doubt you go back to what God said to you. You talk to yourself. Do I believe this or not? If you have a word from God, you go back to what God told you. Maybe it was a very striking conviction in your heart. It could have been a vision or a dream that was vividly confirmed to you. It could have been a Scripture which you were reading and which was amazingly appropriate to your situation and you felt sure it came from God. Go back to the 'word' that God gave you. If you are still in doubt, you can always ask God for a confirmation. Refuse to waver. What you need is a clear word from God. You can talk to God about your doubts, as Abraham did (Gen. 15:3). You can ask for a confirmation. God sees when we need help and will give us a confirmation of his will when we need it.

It is not uncommon, when God is about to do something great, for us to have to face great difficulties. Obstacles may rise up in front of us that are immense. But if we know that we have received a word from God we shall be able to face the obstacles without despair. When God has promised something we do not necessarily have to find ways and means for God's will to come to pass. He can raise the dead, he can create what was not there before. As long as we are sure that he has spoken to us, we shall be alright. We can be strong and say, 'I believe that it shall be just as it was told to me.'

32

The Strengthening of Faith
(Romans 4:20)

Faith gets stronger by glorifying God.

Paul says, '. . . he was strengthened in faith, by giving glory to God' (Rom. 4:20). At first sight it is not clear whether Paul's Greek phrase is saying Abraham 'was strengthened *by* faith' or that Abraham 'was strengthened *in* faith'. However Paul has just used the phrase 'without becoming weak *in* faith' and has said Abraham 'did not waver *in* unbelief'. So if he has used the words '*in* faith . . . *in* unbelief', he must surely be continuing the same idea, and the best translation is 'he was strengthened *in* faith'. His faith was getting stronger as he gave glory to God.

Actually it comes down to the same thing because when one is strengthened in one's faith one then finds that one is strong oneself! First one becomes strengthened in faith and then the faith makes one strong to go out and do great things for God with boldness. When our faith is strong, we are strong, because we are strong in God. When our faith is strengthened, we are strengthened.

Paul's words, 'he was strengthened in faith', imply at least four things.

1. There is such a thing as weak faith, faith that needs strengthening.
2. There is such a thing as strong faith, faith that has grown strong.
3. There is such a thing as growing faith, or faith being strengthened.
4. What leads to the growth of faith is giving glory to God.

Let us consider each of them.

There is such a thing as weak faith.

There are degrees of faith. The strength of one's faith is a matter of how much one reasons out and applies one's faith. There may come times of doubt and uncertainty. There can be variation in the boldness of our faith. Little faith consists of a failure to follow through and apply the faith that one has. Little faith is faith that does not glorify God in critical situations.

Anxiety comes because of little faith (Matt. 6:30). The remedy is to apply the faith one has to the particular situation. Little faith is faith in the earliest saving promises of God, but faith that is not applied when a crisis comes. Saving faith is faith for one's eternal salvation. It is a basic confidence that God means what he says. But this basic faith is only weak faith if it stays at that point.

The panic of the disciples in a storm was caused by little faith (Matt. 8:26). They never said to themselves, 'Jesus has saved us. We have seen him do wonderful things. We have seen him show us many times that he can do the most amazing miracles. So now that we are in this crisis we can surely trust him'. This is what they did not say. Little faith fails to apply what it knows to the new situation.

Peter's panic when walking on the water was caused by little faith (Matt. 14:31). He did not say to himself, 'Jesus has brought me this far. I trusted in him and this is what he enabled me to do. If he enabled me for the first few steps on the water, he will enable me for the rest'. Again, this is what he did not say. Small faith fails to follow through on what God has done so far.

The disciples' pessimism when having no food was a matter of little faith (Matt. 16:8). Jesus asks them, 'Don't you remember the five loaves for the five thousand?' (Matt. 16:9). They were worrying about having no food, but a little bit of spiritual logic would have increased their faith. Small faith is when we do not remember what God has done and do not make any deductions from the faithfulness of what he has done in the past. Strong faith is applied faith; weak faith is unapplied faith.

At one stage Abraham had weak faith. It was weak faith when he was questioning whether God really would give him a seed ('Look, you have not given a seed to me', Gen. 15:3). It was weak faith and a turning to the flesh when Abraham tried to get the seed born by making use of Hagar (Gen. 16:1–4). At that point he was failing to apply what he had already learned about God.

There is such a thing as strong faith.

Strong faith is faith that has overcome doubts. 'If you have faith and do not doubt . . . you can say to this mountain "Go, throw yourself into the sea", and it will be done. If you believe, you will receive whatever you ask for in prayer' (Matt. 21:21). This is strong faith, faith without doubting. Mark 11:22–25 puts it even more strongly. James 1:5–7 refers to praying for wisdom and adds, 'But let him ask in faith, not doubting anything. For he who doubts is like a wave of the sea . . . Let not that man suppose that he shall receive anything from the Lord. . . .' Strong faith is faith without doubting.

There is such a thing as the growth of faith, or faith being strengthened.

Paul says of Abraham, 'he was strengthened in faith'.

What leads to the growth of faith is giving glory to God.

Abraham remembered what God was like. Then he considered the character of God. He said to himself, 'I know that God can do anything. He can create things from nothing. He can raise the dead.' He remembered the faithfulness of God. He said in effect, 'God has never let me down. He has never said something to me which has turned out to be false. I know I can utterly rely on him.' Then he remembered the truthfulness of God. He said, 'God never lies. He has given me this promise, and if he has said that I shall be the father of many nations then I can believe that it will be so. God never lies. He has given his word and I know that it is utterly trustworthy.'

This is what it means to glorify God and when we hold on to God in this way we become strengthened in faith.

33

Fully Persuaded (Romans 4:20–21)

Faith gets stronger by glorifying God. Think of the Canaanite woman of Matthew 15:21–28. She puts a request to Jesus but the response is discouraging (15:21–26). Jesus seems to ignore her. The disciples reject her. Jesus is not called at that time to minister to gentiles. She has nothing to encourage her. What does she do? She glorifies God! In this case, she holds on to Jesus' mercy. Even a dog is treated with mercy and is thrown a crumb or two. She knows Jesus has the power. She believes Jesus will be merciful. So she holds on to what she knows about God and his mercy in Jesus and refuses to give up. She even argues with Jesus.

Jesus is delighted. 'Woman, you have great faith,' he says. This is what great faith is. It is faith that lays hold of the character of God, that refuses to give up, that grows strong by insisting that God is what he says he is and does what he says he will do.

There is a similar incident in Matthew 8:5–13. The centurion asked for his servant to be healed. Again he glorifies God. This time he glorifies the authority of Jesus. He says, 'I know all about authority. Where there is real authority you only have to speak a word and things happen. Jesus, I know you have authority. . . .' He is glorifying God. He is not looking to himself or thinking about himself. He is laying hold of what he knows Jesus is like. Jesus calls it 'great faith' (Matt. 8:10) and it is rewarded by his getting what he asked for (Matt. 8:13). It was this greatness of faith that characterized Abraham. Although everything was against him, he persisted in believing boldly and confidently that God had the power to do what he had promised.

Romans 4:21 draws Paul's description of strong faith to a close. Abraham was strengthened in faith, by giving glory to God, *and by being persuaded that the one who promised was able also to perform*.

Verse 20 speaks generally; verse 21 mentions two details. In general, Abraham glorified God's power and graciousness. In particular, Abraham was convinced that God's word was serious ('the one who had promised') and that God had the power to keep his promise ('. . . was able also to perform'). Again we see how faith has to relate to God's word. Abraham was holding on to 'one who promised', one who had given a word. But we can note two other aspects of faith.

Faith is totally outward looking.

Faith is not some virtue that we possess. It is not pretending or acting as though we believed something when we in fact do not believe it. Faith looks away from itself. It is not self-conscious. God says, 'Look unto me' (Isa. 45:22).

Faith is an ever-intensifying persuasion of the heart about God and his will.

There is what we could call an initial persuasion and what we could call a full persuasion. Faith is a strong conviction that what God has said is utterly true, so that one can base one's life and all one's expectations on what God has said. Faith is assurance about God. It is 'being sure' of what we hope for. It is being 'certain' of what we do not see (Heb. 11:1).

However I hasten to add that faith is not necessarily being sure of ourselves. We may look to God and be sure that there is mercy and answer in him and yet at the same time feel unsure of ourselves. Faith is a conviction that God means what he says and that we can act upon the truth of what he has said.

Faith may begin simply as an assurance about God and there may not be much assurance about ourselves. Yet as faith becomes strong it is assurance about ourselves as well. As we lean on God we know that we are safe. We are able to say, 'I know whom I have believed and I am persuaded. . . .' We end up having no fears at all about our particular need or situation. Faith like this makes us willing to speak. 'I believed; therefore have I spoken' (2 Cor. 4:13). Faith may begin by being a mixture of strength and weakness. It may be assurance about God but doubt about ourselves. But faith rises to fuller and greater confidence.

We may want to ask the question: how can we have faith like this? I come back to the point that Paul keeps on emphasizing. Faith needs a word from God. We can believe anything if we know that God has spoken to us. 'Abraham believed God . . . ' (Rom. 4:3). He believed because something was spoken to him (Rom. 4:17a). 'Against hope but in hope Abraham believed in order that he would become a father of many nations, according to what had been spoken' (Rom. 4:18). 'He did not waver in unbelief in his attitude to the promise of God' (4:20). 'He was persuaded that the one who had promised was able also to perform' (4:21). Again and again Paul emphasizes that it was the promise to Abraham that enabled him to rise to such heights.

If we are to get to our inheritance in the way that Abraham 'by faith and patience' inherited what God was promising him, we need a word from God. We need to have God speak to us. We need to know God's will. Faith is not working ourselves up to claim things that God is not wanting to do. Faith is knowing God, hearing his voice, and laying hold of what we know is his will in our lives. We can do anything if we know God's will. This kind of faith comes from a life lived in the presence of God, a life of prayerfulness and of deep trust in God. As we live a life with God, talking to him, listening to him, approaching him constantly through Jesus, we get to know God's will and God's ways. We can trust him. He proves himself to us again and again. We grow strong in faith and we inherit the promises.

34

Inheriting Faith, Justifying Faith
(Romans 4:22–24a)

At this point Paul turns aside from his remarks about inheritance and comes back to speak of justification again. He does not even finish his account of Abraham's faith. One expects Paul to say, 'And being persuaded that the one who had promised was also able to perform, his faith was rewarded and Isaac was born, and so he inherited the promise by his faith.' But actually he does not bother to finish off his account of Abraham's inheritance of the promise. Paul's purpose at the beginning of the chapter was to convince us that we are justified through faith in Jesus and in no other way. He turned aside slightly in verse 13 to make the point that it is only through being justified that we are able to persist in faith and reach our inheritance as Abraham did. His main point was not to talk about inheritance but to make the point that it is only faith that inherits. The same faith that justifies goes on to inherit God's promises. It is through standing before God with a reckoned righteousness that we are able to persist in faith and so get to our inheritance.

Remember that justice and inheritance are not the same. We may itemize six differences.

1. Justification is an initial blessing of the Christian life; inheritance is an eventual blessing.
2. Justification comes with one's first faith; inheritance comes by persistent faith.
3. Justification opens the way for inheritance; inheritance is the goal of justification, its 'fulfilment'.
4. Justification cannot be lost; inheritance may be lost.
5. Justification relates to acceptance; inheritance relates to ministry and calling.
6. Justification is by faith alone; inheritance comes by persisting in faith and there will always be works of faith.

Paul now turns the argument around and makes the opposite point to the one he has been making so far. Hitherto he has been saying that the faith that justifies is the faith that inherits. Now, still with Abraham in mind, he makes the opposite point. The faith that inherited such a mighty blessing as the birth of Isaac was the same faith that he had in Genesis 15:6, the same faith with which he was justified. *So then it* – this faith of his – *was reckoned to him for righteousness*. His opening word is a weak word, and is not the usual one for 'therefore', which is stronger. We could paraphrase, 'Now then it is this faith that was reckoned to him for righteousness.' Paul is linking the faith that he has been speaking of (4:17–21) with the faith that had been mentioned earlier in the Abraham story (Gen. 15:6, quoted in Rom. 4:1–5). Justifying faith and inheriting faith are the same faith. Initially faith justifies; eventually faith inherits. But it is the same faith. This very faith that achieved so much in Abraham's life was the faith that had in its earliest beginnings been reckoned to Abraham for righteousness. So Paul says, *So then it was reckoned to him for righteousness* (Rom. 4:22).

He continues: *And it was not written on his account only that it was reckoned to him.* Why was the story of Abraham written up in the book of Genesis in such detail? Paul has a particular view of the Old Testament here in this verse. In his mind the Old Testament is not just a random and accidental collection of stories and writings. It is part of God-breathed Scripture and came together in a way that God intended. There is a purpose in the way his story has come down to us in written form. Paul can say, 'It was not just for the sake of Abraham.' It was not simply that someone liked the idea of writing up the story of Abraham because it was interesting, or because it made a good start for someone with ambitions as a writer. No, when the story of Abraham came into being and was preserved down the centuries, there was a purpose for future generations of the people of God. It was not written on his account only . . . *but also it was written on our account* (Rom. 4:24).

God planned from the very beginning that Abraham might be a model for the entire world and for the rest of human history. Abraham is the classic example of how to be justified. Everything about the Abraham story is fitted to be a sample of what is and what is not the way of salvation. His being justified without the law centuries before Moses was deliberate and was intended by God. His justification before his circumcision was deliberate and intended by God. God always planned it that at one stage of his life Abraham should be equivalent to a gentile in that he was uncircumcised, and Jews regarded uncircumcised people as gentiles. At another stage of his life Abraham was equivalent to a circumcised Jew. The reason why, in the will of God, the story of Abraham was written up and Genesis 15:6 was included in the books of the law that came into being at the time of Moses was so that it might be a standing account for the whole of human history of the way of salvation for all people, Jews and gentiles.

It is interesting that it is Abraham and not Noah who was the one God chose. Actually the first person after Adam who came to salvation was Abel and the first person who is said to have 'found grace' was Noah. He was brought to salvation just like Abraham. But Noah and a few others were chosen and brought safely through God's judgment, and the rest of the world was condemned. Abraham was chosen for a different reason and was destined to be used in a different way. He was not the first one to be justified, but he was the first one God chose to use as a model and prototype for the rest of the world. Abraham is the model of salvation, the model of inheritance, the 'father of us all'. His way of justification is *the* way of justification.

35

Faith in Christ Crucified
(Romans 4:24–25)

The story of Abraham was written for all Abraham's spiritual children. It was written on our account also. *It was written for us to whom it would be reckoned, to us who believe on the one who raised Jesus our Lord from the dead* (Rom. 4:24), *Jesus who was delivered up because of our transgression and was raised because of our justification* (Rom. 4:25).

With these words Paul summarizes and brings to a close everything he has been saying since Romans 3:21, before proceeding to a major forward move in his letter, in Romans 5:1. All of the major elements of his teaching concerning atonement and justification are here in these few lines.

1. Salvation is a matter of justification, a matter of righteousness being reckoned ours. The story of Abraham is to help God's people stay clear and lucid concerning this matter. It was written 'on our account . . . for us to whom righteousness would be reckoned'. These phrases add nothing new to Paul's teaching but they summarize and remind us of what he has said in Romans 3:21–4:22.
2. Salvation becomes ours by faith and by faith only. The Abraham story, Paul says, makes it clear. It enables us to

know for certain that faith and faith only is the way of salvation. Jewishness does not come into it. Works of the law do not come into it. No kind of 'works' is the way of justification in Paul's sense of the term. Works of faith no doubt enter in at a later stage as the outworking of our faith while we are on our way to our inheritance. But works do not come into justification itself in Paul's sense of the term. (James' use of the term is different and does not refer to initial salvation.) Abraham's story is 'written for us . . . us who believe . . . '.

3. Paul reminds us of what he said back in Romans 3:24. Justification is 'through the redemption that is in Christ Jesus'. In Abraham's case, he was believing on the promise connected with the coming of Jesus. In our case the promised one has arrived, he is 'now . . . manifested' (Rom. 3:21). So we, like Abraham, believe on 'Jesus our Lord', but we know the name 'Jesus' whereas Abraham did not.

4. Like Abraham we believe in 'God'. But it is not any 'god'. It is specifically the one who promised the seed to Abraham, the one who (as we now know more clearly) 'raised Jesus our Lord from the dead'. We do not believe only in Jesus. We must not imagine that somehow Jesus is the Saviour but the Father is the one we need to be saved from. That is not the right way to put it. 'God – God the Father! – so loved the world that he sent his one and only Son . . . ' (John 3:16). We believe in 'God our Saviour' (1 Tim. 1:1). 'God commended his love towards us. . . .'

God was at work when he sent Jesus to the cross. God

was acting when he raised Jesus from the dead. We
believe in this message of what God was doing in and
through his Son.

5. We also believe that 'Jesus' is 'Lord'. Our faith knows
who Jesus is. He is the Lord! When we put our trust in
Jesus we are putting our trust in the entire message
concerning Jesus. We know about 'God' – the God of
Abraham, the God of the Old Testament, the God of
Jesus. We know about Jesus and we know who he is.
Jesus the Lord! We know what happened to him. God
the Father laid our sins upon him. We know he was
raised from the dead. The Abraham story 'was written
for us . . . who believe on the one who raised Jesus our
Lord . . . '.

6. Paul's way of putting the matter reminds us of what it
was that made this gospel message necessary. It was
'because of our transgressions' that Jesus was delivered
up. Paul has used various words for 'sin' throughout his
letter so far. He has spoken of 'ungodliness' and 'un-
righteousness' (1:18). He has spoken of 'sin' (3:20) and
'sins' (3:25) and 'lawlessnesses' (4:7, a more literal translation). Then in Romans 4:15 he spoke of the way in
which the law turned 'sins' into 'transgressions'. This is
the strongest word of all. It means sin that is deliberate,
sin that crosses a limit where God has said, 'no entry'.
Romans 4:25 uses again the word 'transgressions'.

We have all been guilty of 'transgressions'. There have
been times where sin has been quite deliberate. We were
running in the opposite direction from the will of God and

we knew it. There was our pride, our covetousness and greed, our impurity, our envy and jealousy, our misuse of the blessings of this world, our anger and bad temper, our laziness and self-centredness. Jesus was delivered up for these aspects of our lives which were so repulsive to God and which Paul summarizes as 'transgressions'. The Father took the transgressions of the entire human race and he laid them on Jesus. Jesus 'carried our sins in his body on the tree' (1 Pet. 2:24). Then the Father poured out his anger towards those sins of ours. No one will ever understand it: Jesus swallowed up all of the anger of God towards those 'transgressions'.

What we do now is trust God in the same way that Abraham trusted God. God spoke; Abraham believed. God said, 'I am giving you a seed'; Abraham believed it. It was as simple as that. We do exactly the same. God speaks. He says, 'I am giving you a Saviour.' We believe it. He says, 'Your sins were laid on Jesus.' We believe it. He says, 'I am giving you the righteousness of Jesus.' We simply take God at his word. Immediately we are clothed with the right-eousness of Jesus Christ. Our lives are changed forever. Then we persist in this faith, standing before God in the righteousness of Jesus and moving towards our inheritance, still by persistent faith in Jesus. And we inherit all of the promises of God for our lives.

36

Christ Risen (Romans 4:25)

Paul speaks of 'Jesus who was delivered over because of our transgressions and was raised because of our justification.' In this way he speaks of the problem of the human race: transgressions. He speaks of the greatness of God's love. It was the Father who 'did not spare his own Son but delivered him up for us all' (Rom. 8:32).

Paul goes on to speak of the effectiveness of what Jesus did on the cross. Jesus was delivered up because of our transgressions but was 'raised because of our justification' (Rom. 4:25).

The translation has been disputed. Is it 'delivered up with a view to (dealing with) our trespasses and raised with a view to our justification'? This is not a very natural translation of the Greek.

Or does the word change its meaning in the middle of the sentence: 'delivered up because of our trespasses and raised with a view to our justification'? Does 'because of' change its meaning mid-sentence?

Another possibility is to translate 'delivered up because of our sins and raised because of our justification'.

This is best, in my opinion. The parallelism should be taken seriously:

'delivered-up   because-of   our-trespasses
raised   because-of   our-justification'.

The words in the middle (one word in Greek) should be given the same meaning throughout. People have some-times been puzzled by the phrase 'raised because of our justification' but actually it is similar to the teaching of Paul elsewhere. Later Paul will say: 'as through one man's trespass something happened for all people for their con-demnation, so also through one man's righteous act some-thing happened for all people for justification of life. For as through the disobedience of one man the many [that is, "everyone"] were constituted sinners, so also through the obedience of the one man the many [that is, "everyone"] will be constituted righteous' (Rom. 5:19,20).

'Justification' has been provided for the entire human race through the death and resurrection of Jesus. Christ's resurrection is the proof that justification has been achieved and is therefore available for the entire human race. Jesus was 'raised because of our justification'. Not every person actually takes that justification by faith in Jesus, but justifi-cation is there for him or her. We shall come back to this again later.

The Christian is justified by Jesus' blood (Rom. 5:9). He or she is justified by faith (Rom. 3:28; 5:1). He or she is justified by grace (Rom. 3:24; Tit. 3:7). And he or she is justified by the resurrection (Rom. 4:25). All four statements are true.

The resurrection proves that Jesus is indeed who and what he claimed to be.

On one occasion Jewish people asked Jesus for a sign to prove his claims. He replied, 'An evil and an adulterous generation seeks for a sign, but no sign shall be given them except the sign of the prophet Jonah' (Matt. 12:39). He went on, 'as Jonah was three days and three nights in the belly of the sea-monster, so shall the Son of Man be three days and three nights in the heart of the earth.' The only sign of his genuineness that Jesus ever gives is himself! He is the sign! As God's Saviour risen from the dead he himself is the sign and the proof that he is the Saviour. John 2:18,19 makes the same point. 'What sign have you to show us?', they asked. 'Destroy this temple, and in three days I will raise it up,' Jesus replied. It was an obscure remark. He was not trying to 'prove' himself in a way that dispensed with faith. But to those who believe, the resurrection vindicates the claims of Jesus. Before the disciples realized that Jesus was raised from the dead, they entirely gave up hope in his being the Redeemer. 'We had hoped that he was the one who would redeem Israel,' was all they could say (Luke 24:21). They were calling him simply 'Jesus of Nazareth . . . a prophet' (Luke 24:19) but that was all that they could say. It was the resurrection that made the entire Old Testament Scriptures fall into place (Luke 24:25–27, 32–35).

The resurrection proves that the condemning power of death has been contested and defeated.

'The wages of sin is death.' Men and women ought to die because death is the penalty of sin and all have sinned. So in a sense death is right to claim the sinner for itself. In some mysterious way – I do not claim to understand it – Jesus submitted himself temporarily to the claims of death. He said to the evil powers behind death, 'This is your hour and the power of darkness.' But then death could not hold him! He was not abandoned to Hades, the realm and reign of death. His flesh suffered no decay (Acts 2:31). Death was a form of punishment and condemnation. Jesus broke its power. Death is punishment; resurrection is release from punishment. Death is condemnation; resurrection is justification, the opposite of condemnation.

The resurrection is the proof that God was satisfied with the cross.

If Jesus had not been raised from the dead we would never quite be sure whether he was indeed a sacrifice for our sins. But the return of Jesus from the grave is the sign that God was pleased with him and had accepted everything he did. Without the resurrection a question mark would have been left hanging over the cross. Was it just a tragic accident? Did it really atone for sins? Did it really provide justification? The resurrection was needed to answer these questions. In the resurrection 'God exalted him at his right hand' (Acts 5:31) to give forgiveness – and justification – to all who believe. Justification was with Jesus. He was vindicated. He was declared righteous. When we believe in Jesus we share his righteousness. We are righteous in Jesus. Justification is 'in Christ' (Gal. 2:17). He was raised because of our justification.

37

Justified by Christ's Resurrection (Romans 4:25)

The resurrection is the occasion of Jesus' having fully dealt with the entire kingdom of sin.

Jesus was 'raised because of our justification'. Paul goes into this in fuller detail in Romans 6. The death Jesus died, he died to sin once, but the life he lives, he lives to God. Jesus came into the realm of sin. He came to deal with it. He came to take upon himself the sorrows and temptations of sinners. When Jesus died he finished that work of dealing with sin. He died to sin, in that sense. He fully paid for all of the consequences of sin. Never again would he have to die, or come under the weight of sin.

Then he was raised by the Father and was utterly delivered from the realm of the dead. He became the king of the universe. So the resurrection is the occasion when Jesus was totally victorious not simply over a few little problems in this world. He was raised in victory and triumph above the entire kingdom of sin. Now he administers the Father's will. It is not the Father's will to condemn us. Jesus has atoned for sin. The Father is satisfied. The entire realm of

sin and condemnation is defeated and put down. There is
no possibility of a true believer ever being condemned.
Jesus has been raised because our justification is a fact. We
have laid hold of Jesus as our Saviour by faith in him and
obtained that justification in our own lives. Jesus is 'justified'
and sits at the right hand of the Father as king of the
universe. We are justified 'in him', in the risen and glorified
Lord Jesus Christ. He was raised because of our justification.
What a wonderful thing it is to be justified, clothed with
the righteousness of Christ.

It means I can forget my sinful past.

No matter what I may have done, my past wickedness is
gone for ever. No sin from the past will ever arise to
condemn me.

It means that I can pray with boldness.

When I want to pray I know I am unworthy. I do not
deserve that God should take any notice of me. But I am
not going to God's presence in my own name. I am entering
the court of God clothed with the righteousness of Jesus.

It means that I do not have to fear death.

If I were to leave this world now, would I be ready to stand
before God? In a sense I am always ready. What better

preparation could there be than the righteousness of Jesus Christ?

It means that I do not rest on how well I am doing in the Christian life.

There may be times when I do not feel I am doing well. I am a long way short of what I want to be. I would like to be more loving, more generous, more like Jesus, more dedicated. I have a long way to go. Can God really bless someone like me? But I am not standing before God in the name of how well I am doing as a Christian. I am standing before God in the righteousness of Jesus Christ. Jesus is already in heaven. He is righteous before the Father. But he was not raised only for himself. He was raised for me. He was raised because my justification has been secured. I do not have to worry about how well I am doing. I cannot do better than to be in Christ! I come before God in his righteousness. There is no way of improving on that. Yes, I want to serve God more, but my position before the Father does not depend on me at all. It depends on Jesus; Jesus is acceptable to the Father so I am too. I am justified in Christ.

When I sin I need not fear rejection.

I do not want to sin. I would not want to grieve my Saviour or grieve the Holy Spirit and invite the heavenly Father to

chasten me in his love. But one thing I know. My heavenly
Father will not reject me. I am covered with the righteousness of his Son! I make holiness complete in the fear of God
(2 Cor. 7:1) but that fear does not involve fear of rejection.
It is rather fear of missing the great things that he wants to
do for me. A person clothed with the righteousness of Jesus
cannot be rejected by God. God does not reject Jesus or
send him away; and I am in Christ.

I can answer the attacks of the devil.

He knows how to accuse. He comes to me at times and
says, 'But what about this – and this – and this.' He knows
how to rake up old sins. He knows how to point to
weaknesses. He loves condemnation and bondage and fear.
But there is one thing Satan cannot do. He cannot overthrow the righteousness of Jesus. He can overthrow my
righteousness. That is very easy for him! But I am not
covered in my righteousness. I am covered in the righteousness of Jesus. So his accusations against my conscience can
be answered. 'You have sinned,' he says. 'But Jesus has died.
Jesus has shed his blood. Jesus has given me his righteousness.' Satan is overcome by the blood of Jesus and by the
word of our testimony.

> A debtor to mercy alone,
> Of covenant mercy I sing;
> Nor fear with God's righteousness on,
> My person and offering to bring.

The terrors of law and of God
With me can have nothing to do;
My Saviour's obedience and blood
Hide all my transgressions from view.

This is a remedy for every trouble, every trial. I am clothed with the righteousness of Jesus Christ. I have a perfect righteousness from a perfect Saviour. What greater security could I have? Thanks be to God for his unspeakable gift.

38

Peace with God (Romans 5:1)

The first result of our trusting in Jesus is that 'we have peace with God through our Lord Jesus Christ'. The first few words of Romans 5 set the theme for Chapters 5 to 8 in the letter to the Romans. He says, *Therefore having been justified by faith we have . . .* That is what this section is all about, the things that 'we have' now that we have been justified by faith.

'Justification' is being 'declared righteous' before God. It is a legal term. Imagine a law court. When the judge pronounces the verdict, if the prisoner is innocent, the judge will declare him or her 'not guilty'. God declares sinners 'not guilty' when they believe in Jesus. Justification is not something done to us; it is a declaration about us. It is when we are clothed with Jesus' righteousness. It has nothing to do with any righteousness that we might have. Jesus' righteousness is 'credited' to us. Romans 3:21–4:25 dealt with the subject of justification. Paul now goes on to deal with what 'therefore' comes to the Christian, now that we have been justified. 'Being justified by faith we have. . . .' This theme continues to the end of Chapter 8.

The four chapters can be viewed as falling into six main sections. In Romans 5:1–11 he is telling us the immediate results of being justified by faith in Jesus. In Romans

5:12–21 he goes on to tell us how this leads to a change of position. Where we once used to be in Adam we now are 'in Christ', and the grace of God rules over us. In Romans 6:1–23 he tells us how this means that we have 'died to sin' and are alive to God in Jesus. Romans 6:1–14 explains our position doctrinally; Romans 6:15–23 comes at the matter more practically. In Romans 7:1–25 he tells us how we have died to the Mosaic law. In Romans 8:1–39 he tells us how we are utterly secure in Christ and can never be condemned.

All of this leads into a final climax. 'What then shall we say to these things?', he asks, and ends the section with a ringing affirmation that nothing can separate us from the love of God in Christ (8:31–39).

Our concern at the moment is with the first few lines. Paul gives us a statement of the things that are immediately true of us, now that we have been justified by faith in Jesus: peace with God (5:1), access into God's grace (5:2a), an expectation of glory (5:2b), an understanding of our troubles (5:3,4), an experience of the love of God (5:5–10) and joy because now in the immediate present we are enjoying reconciliation with God (5:11).

Therefore having been justified by faith we have peace with God through our Lord Jesus Christ (Rom. 5:1). It means that we know that God is satisfied with Jesus' righteousness. The reason why we are justified is that Jesus has lived a sinless life for us, and Jesus has died the death we should have died. Everything has been done. God has been satisfied by the sacrifice of Jesus on the cross. So we can have peace with God. If God is satisfied, we can be satisfied. Our heart is at rest about our relationship to God. We have confidence. We are not nervous about God, not hiding from him in the way that Adam hid himself after his great sin.

It means that we are no more seeking and questing. The Christian is not a person who is 'interested in religion'. He or she is a person who has found a Saviour. He or she is reconciled to God. God is his or her friend. Before we came to know Jesus we were hostile towards God. God had problems with us too. Although he loved us, he was having problems with our sins. He had showed love in creating us in his image, but we did not respond to that love and God became angry. But now all that is finished. We have believed in Jesus. God has looked at us through his Son. He has declared us 'not guilty' in his sight. We know that he is not holding a grudge against us, not looking at us with any ill will. No, he looks at us through Jesus and we are at peace with him.

Until we come to know Jesus we can never really be at ease with God. We will be afraid of God and secretly will be hostile to him. We may like the idea of God, the theory of God, but we fear actually having dealings with the living God himself. All of that disappears when we discover Jesus. Without Jesus we can have a certain kind of carelessness as we walk through life, but we shall never have true peace with God except through Jesus. The Pharisee, the religious churchgoer who is moral and upright but has never found Jesus, does not really have peace. The false convert does not have it. The person who walks forward at an evangelistic appeal, hoping that something might happen but without faith in Jesus in their heart will find that their 'decision'

brings them no peace and will not do so until they personally trust Jesus. It is 'our Lord Jesus Christ' himself who
brings peace.

If we look to Jesus alone we shall find true peace in him.
Look to Jesus alone! Know that he has lived the life you
should have lived. Know that he has died the death you
should have died. Know that the Father has accepted his
death upon the cross. Everything else in this section of
Romans begins here. There is no power over sin without
peace with God first.

In Jerusalem, on the day when Jesus rose from the dead,
he appeared suddenly in the room and showed them his
hands and his side. It was as if he was saying, 'I know that
you betrayed me and abandoned me when I needed you,
but it is alright! I died for you. Look at the hands which
they pierced. I was dying for your sins. Look at my side
from where my blood flowed. It was flowing for you. Your
sins have been paid for. The punishment has gone.'

He showed them his hands and his side and he said,
'Peace be with you' (John 20:21). It is still the same. When
we see that Jesus has died for us and put our trust in him
and his cross, we have peace with God through our Lord
Jesus Christ.

39

Access to God's Grace (Romans 5:2a)

After we find peace with God, through Jesus, we have an
entry into God's kingdom of grace. Paul says, *Through him
we have gained access into this grace in which we now stand*. This
is one of the keys to this entire section of Romans: in
Chapters 5 to 8 it will be developed at large. But here is
the starting point. When we believe in Jesus we immediately have a way in to God's grace. Conversion to Jesus
Christ is like a doorway into a palace or into a vast treasure
house. No one is allowed in unless they are clothed with
the righteousness of Jesus. The moment we are clothed with
the righteousness of Jesus we have an access, a way in, to
the vast treasure house of God's grace.

Conversion to Jesus is not only getting our sins forgiven;
it is more than that. Conversion to Jesus Christ must be
thought of as a transfer between two kingdoms. When we
believe in Jesus we are immediately in a new kingdom.
We are 'delivered . . . from the dominion of darkness and
transferred . . . into the kingdom of the Beloved Son'
(Col. 1:13).

It is this theme that Paul is about to develop. This access
into grace is something that has happened to us already and
will last for ever. The translation, 'we have access' is not
strong enough. It is better translated as 'we have obtained

access'. The point is that we have got it! It is ours for ever. God has taken hold of us and transferred us into a new kingdom.

The old realm was characterized by sin but the realm of grace is a realm of freedom from sin. Paul will develop this theme in Chapter 6 of Romans. The old realm was a realm of living up to the law; the realm of grace is living under the powerful activities of the grace of God. We are not 'keeping it up'. The grace of God keeps us up! It takes us through every barrier. It becomes a well of water inside of us springing up into eternal life (John 4:14). The old life was a life under God's wrath and judgment; grace is the continuous experience of his love and mercy. It is an entire realm of mercy, a vast domain where there is such gener-osity. The old realm was a place of death; grace gives life and energy; it gives nourishment and provision. The old life was bondage; the new life is being bound to Jesus, which is freedom. There is true liberty, liberty from sin and guilt, liberty to be truly ourselves under the leadings of God's Holy Spirit. The old life was a life of sinful works or works of law or works arising from how guilty we felt. The new life does not arise from guilt. It springs up in our hearts out of gratitude. We serve God. We pay attention to good works. But they are works of faith. Works of love. Works of optimism.

The old life was characterized by decay. It was what Paul will call 'the old person' (Rom. 6:7). It was backward looking. It was humanity 'in Adam' who brought the human race into ruin. It did not hold out hope for anything new. But the kingdom of grace is ever new! We walk in

newness of life. We have put on 'the new person' (Eph.
4:24) which is freshly created according to the image of
God, who is love and holiness and purity. The old life was
'flesh', weak, decaying humanity. The new kingdom of
grace is 'righteousness and peace and joy in the Holy Spirit'
(Rom. 14:17). We have the ever-flowing newness of the
Holy Spirit. The old was condemnation; the new is acceptance. When we trust in Jesus and in so doing step over into
the kingdom of God's grace, in that very split second 'we
have obtained' our access into this grace.

And we stand there. Paul speaks of our having access
'into this grace in which we now stand'. We stand! It partly
means that God keeps us. As Paul will put it later: 'he will
stand, for the Lord is able to make him stand' (Rom. 14:4).
Does this lead to sin? Paul will answer that very question:
can we go on in sin so that grace may abound? And he will
answer the question by giving us an even bigger picture of
grace! No, no! We have been placed into Jesus. Grace has
caused us to die to sin. We shall not find we can easily go
on in the life of sin. If we try God is able to deal with us.
Grace trains us in godliness (Tit. 2:11,12).

But this phrase, 'in which we stand', means that we are
confident about it. 'The Lord is able to cause us to stand'
– and so we do. We do not slouch in grace. We do not
stoop or droop. We do not slouch or slither. We stand! The
Christian life is a life of boldness and confidence. It is not
confidence in ourselves but it is confidence in God. What
Paul was wanting his friends to see was that they – and we
– have such grounds for confidence in Jesus. The amazing
grace of God will keep us. We are released from our old

life. We have already obtained our access into grace. We are there! We have arrived! Admittedly, there is a little bit of mopping up of the old life to be done. There are a few hangovers from the old humanity. We are still in a mortal body, we still have the flesh. Though we are 'seated in the heavenly places' in our position, we have a little experience of this world to be gone through before we fully enjoy our glory in heaven. But basically we are there. 'We have obtained access by faith into this grace in which we now stand!'

40

The Glory of God (Romans 5:2b)

The next result of being right with God that Paul mentions is our expectation of the glory of God: . . . *and we rejoice in our expectation of the glory of God* (Rom. 5:26).

Because we are justified, clothed with the righteousness of Jesus, we can have peace with God. We know we are in God's realm of grace. Also we have a great delight in knowing that we are going to be partakers in the glory of God. The word 'hope', as some translations have it, does not refer to any kind of doubtful desire that maybe something will happen. We sometimes use the word that way. 'I hope to visit my parents,' we say. We mean it might be possible, it might not. But that is not the way the word is used in the Bible. It does not mean 'hope' in that sense. It means expectation, anticipation, looking forward to something we know will come.

What is the glory of God? It is the outshining of his holiness. It is when his powerful purity is in some way visible. It shines out in heaven. Partial glimpses of it were seen by Moses (Exod. 33) and by the disciples on the mountain of transfiguration (Matt. 17:2) and by Stephen (Acts 7:55).

The human race was made in the image of God. Whether Adam literally had any light shining round him like a halo,

I do not know. But there was a 'glory' about him. If you had been there you would have been able to see the righteousness of God in which he was created.

But the human race lost its glory. 'All have sinned and lack the glory of God' (Rom. 3:23), the outshining of God's holy character that we are meant to share.

It is this glory that brings us honour. When there is a visible outshining of our holiness it brings us honour. Because glory is radiation, outshining, it is seen. Others admire it. I believe this is one reason why we all love so much the praise of other people. It is that we are yearning for our lost glory, craving for every little bit of honour we can get. Unfortunately we look for glory in the wrong way, and our doing so blocks up the flowing of faith in our lives. 'How can you believe when you are receiving glory from one another and not seeking glory from the only God?' (John 5:44). But the Christian is rejoicing in the expectation of the glory of God. People may take our honour from us in this world. We can be put down before other people. We can come to the end of a famous career. If we have been looking for glory from men and women we shall be mournful people when we do not get it.

But the Christian's hope can be put into one phrase: the glory of God. When Jesus comes what will be seen is his glory. When we get to heaven, it will be a place of glory. Everything radiates with the glory of God. We shall 'behold his glory' (John 17:24). The Christian will be 'made perfect' when he or she is taken to heaven (Heb. 12:23) and will enter a place of the outshining glory of God. But at the resurrection his or her very body will be glorified, and will shine out with the holiness of God. Our bodies will be 'raised in glory' (1 Cor. 15:43).

This glorification has a lot to do with our reward in heaven, because there will be levels of glory. This is obviously a difficult matter to understand. We shall know far more about it when we get there. But the Bible says that 'one star differs from another star in glory; so it is with the resurrection of the dead' (1 Cor. 15:41,42). Earlier in that very same epistle Paul speaks of different levels of reward, and of each person receiving his praise from God (1 Cor. 3:10–15; 4:5). How do we receive praise from God? In heaven it is partly audible. Jesus will speak and give his 'well done' over everything we have done for him. But it is also visible. Our level of holiness will shine out.

However in Romans 5:2 the emphasis is not on the variety of glory but simply on the fact that every Christian will get there. Jesus is bringing many sons to glory (Heb. 2:10).

This great day when we shall be 'glorified' will be a corporate event. We shall all enter into our glory together. What a wonderful joint celebration it will be. How we shall admire each other without jealousy!

There is another aspect to this 'glory'. It is not only the glory of God seen, and the glory of our holiness experienced, the glory of our bodies visible. It is also the glorification of creation. It is a renewed heavens and earth (2 Pet. 2:12,13). It is when the corruption of our present world is done away with (Rom. 8:18–24).

The point Paul is making in Romans 5:2 is that it is because we are justified that we can look forward to the glory of God in this way. We would never be sure we were going to heaven if we were not clothed with righteousness. Indeed, at this point, we do not so much need to have levels of glory in mind. Paul's concern is that we are rejoicing in the sheer fact that we are to get there. If you believe in Jesus you are going to get to see and experience the glory of God. It is so certain that you can start rejoicing in it right away. It ought to motivate your life, the thought that the holiness given to you in Jesus and worked out in the very way you live is going to shine out in heaven. If we know what it is to be justified we start rejoicing immediately. We are going to see and to share in the glory of God!

41

Trials and Tribulations (Romans 5:3–4)

In Romans 5:1–2 Paul leaps from justification to glorifica-tion. If we are justified, we shall be glorified (compare Rom. 8:30). We might want to ask the question, what about everything in between? What about the holy life? What about the trials and testings we go through? Paul does not deal with them at first. They make no difference! Sin will not have dominion over us (Rom. 6:14); we shall be brought through every trial (see Rom. 0.33–39). Those whom God justified, he also glorified.

However we do need to know how to face times of trouble and where the godly life fits in, so Paul comes to that next. He says: *And not only that, but we also rejoice in our tribulations. . . .* It is not just that we rejoice in the wonderful things such as our first salvation and our getting to glory. We also rejoice in the very practical and tough matter of facing the hardships and sudden calamities of life.

Firstly, we must realize that tough times will come.

We must not have that view of the Christian life and of salvation that gives the impression that Jesus takes all problems away. Even worse, we must not hold to any kind of 'health and wealth' gospel that says it is impossible (or sinful) for the Christian to be sick or in financial need or in any kind of trouble. That is quite against the Word of God. We have victory over every problem. But God can give us that victory either by taking the problem away in his time, or by giving us grace to endure and triumph, as in 2 Corinthians 12:7–10. Paul knows that we shall have tribulations or sufferings. 'In the world you have troubles, but be courageous, I have overcome the world' (John 16:33). 'It is by means of many troubles that we must enter the kingdom of God' (Acts 14:22).

However, secondly, we are able to rejoice in tribulations.

It is not that we rejoice in the troubles themselves. No one enjoys trouble in itself, and God does not ask that of us. What Paul says is that we rejoice, 'knowing . . . '. We do not rejoice in the trouble itself. But we rejoice because there is some-thing that we know. We know that God is using these troubles of ours to mould us, and we rejoice in that. We do not grumble. It is not that we simply endure them and rejoice despite the distresses of life. We positively rejoice because we know what God is doing. We are given an understanding of the distresses that God puts us through, no matter what they may be. James says the same thing. '**Consider it a matter of joy, my brothers and sisters, when you fall into various testings, because you 'know . . . '** (James 1:2).

Thirdly, our troubles powerfully lead us to the godly life.

They have a strong effect on us. This is the answer to the question that we might have been asking when Paul leapt from justification to glorification. Does not God intend to lead us into holiness in between our salvation and our getting to glory? Yes he does. Tribulations of various kinds are one way in which he does it. And our reaction to troubles will determine how fast we grow in holiness.

How does it work? Troubles work perseverance. Paul says, *we rejoice in our tribulations, knowing that tribulation works perseverance. . . .* What is this perseverance? It is the determination to carry on. It is toughness. It is constancy. It is the determination that we are going to serve the Lord, come what may. It is pressing on with God. You never develop this determination to press on with God until you have a few troubles and testings.

Then troubles lead us on to character. Paul says, *tribulation works perseverance,* (Rom. 5:3) *and perseverance works character, and character works hope* (Rom. 5:4). This word 'character' means the quality of having faced a test and passed it. It means 'proven quality'. It takes a few testings for a person to develop a strong character for Jesus.

I have sometimes made a friendship with someone whose life I can tell is a life of prayer, or great dedication or sincerity or zeal for Jesus. Such people are often unostentatious, almost hidden people. But I like to have as my friends people who know much of Jesus, people whose spirituality you can feel. I have sometimes asked, 'Tell me,

John' – or Joan or Jack or Mary or whatever – 'how did you get to be the way you are?' They have normally been a bit embarrassed and I have said, 'Come on, we have become good friends and you obviously know the Lord. How did you get to know Jesus in the way you do?' If they have been willing to share with me, the answer has always been the same. Godly people have always had some serious and heavy troubles that they have been through. Often there has been a 'Judas' in their life and they have had to learn the secret of forgiveness. Sometimes they were widowed in the most distressing circumstances. Sometimes they were desperately needy, more needy than most people can ever conceive. Perseverance in the ways of God amidst testing circumstances works proven character.

Troubles lead on to hope. The problem with all of us is that we are so earthly minded. It needs a few troubles or disappointments before we really start looking forward to the glory Paul mentioned in verse 2. We get very excited about the world, about our wealth maybe, or our successes, our fame or our pleasures, until a few troubles start coming our way. Then we are challenged and pulled up sharp. We start asking ourselves, 'What am I really living for?' And we are led to fix our eyes on where God is taking us, to our final glory. Then on top of that is the outpoured love of God.

42

Love Poured Out (Romans 5:5)

Our troubles may intensify our expectation of glory.

For our very distresses can help us to think clearly about
what we are living for, and can get us to stretch forward
towards the blessings that come to us in the new heavens
and new earth. We begin with hope (verse ?) but in troubles
hope gets intensified and brings about a deeper hope.

This hope is not just a theory; it does not fade away. Paul
says, *And hope does not prove disappointing, because the love of
God is poured out in our hearts by the Holy Spirit whom he has
given to us* (Rom. 5:5). There are many hopes that disap-
point us. We have expectations of great successes that we
think are coming, but after a while they fade and our hopes
wither.

There is an experience that keeps hope flourishing.

Something takes place in the Christian's heart which prevents expectations of glory from withering. It is the 'love

of God poured out in our hearts by the Holy Spirit who was given to us'.

What is this outpouring of the love of God? I think I could call it an ongoing 'baptism' in the love of God. The term Paul uses here, 'poured out', is the term normally associated with the day of Pentecost. Isaiah predicted a day when the Spirit would be 'poured out' from on high (Isa. 32:15) and said God promised, 'I will pour out my Spirit' (Isa. 44:3). Ezekiel and Zechariah gave similar promises (Ezek. 39:29; Zech. 12:10). Joel is famous for the promise, 'I will pour out my Spirit' (Joel 2:28,29). The word is used in connection with the events of Acts 2, which speaks of 'the promise of the Father' (Acts 1:5; see also 2:38), being 'baptized with the Spirit' (Acts 1:5), 'receiving power' (Acts 1:8) and being 'filled' (Acts 2:4); then it is called the 'outpouring of the Spirit' (Acts 2:17,18,33). It is not purely a corporate event, because Titus 3:5 speaks of being saved, being justified, receiving regeneration and the renewing of the Spirit, and in that context says God 'poured out the Spirit on us'. Clearly he is referring to personal experience. Neither Paul nor Titus nor the Christians in Crete, where Titus was, were present on the day of Pentecost, but they had all known their own experience of the outpouring of the Spirit in their lives.

Here in Romans we have the idea of a 'baptism' or an 'outpouring' of love which comes by the Holy Spirit.

Is this love of God, poured out in our hearts, baptism with the Spirit? It is closely related, but there is a slight difference. Paul uses the present tense. With a slight exaggeration of the Greek tense we could translate, 'The love of God goes on being poured out. . . .' This is an ongoing experience. The reason why our hope of glory does not prove disappointing to us is that we are conscious that we are being loved and brought to glory. Our hope is not just a theory. We are aware and conscious of being cherished. The love of God is poured out in our hearts. The Greek does not say 'into' our hearts. The Holy Spirit is already there. But having already been given to us, this is a work that he does within our hearts. He pours out a sense of God's love. We are meant to have this all of the time. The first time it ever happens to us we call it 'baptism with the Spirit'. But I would call this an ongoing 'baptism' with the love of God.

There are two ways of knowing the love of God. One way is by logic. Paul comes to that in verses 6 to 10. Notice how argumentative and logical those five verses are. Paul makes deductions from the cross of Jesus, and deductions from the fact that we have been justified. But there is another way of knowing the love of God, and that is by direct experience. But it is the direct experience that enables us to use the logic! He mentions the direct experience first. This is the greatest way of knowing the love of God. It is the Spirit's work to pour out a 'baptism', a 'flood' of the love of God. First comes the direct experience. Then we are able to reason out and argue out our knowledge of the love of God. Because we are justified by faith God is able to pour out a direct experience of his love. We are meant to know this. We shall lose it if we grieve the Spirit. There may be times when God will remove the feeling of his love from us temporarily. But generally speaking we are meant to know the love of God, to feel that God loves us. What is it? I scarcely know how to put it into words. It is when the arguments of Romans 5:6–10 just seem to spring up in our hearts. We can see God loves us. We can feel the sunshine of his face. We know that he is smiling upon us. This is why our expectation of glory does not prove disappointing. This has nothing to do with 'deducing' that God loves us. It is a direct feeling that God loves us. It is given to us by the Spirit. We ought to be enjoying it all of the time. It is not necessarily ecstatic, but it is joyful. We may not dance around the room because of it – but then we might! It is the steady day-by-day feeling that arises in our hearts that God loves us. Our hope of glory does not prove disappointing because by the love of God poured out in our hearts, we have one foot in glory already.

43

The Love of God (Romans 5:5–8)

The love of God is a fact and it is a feeling. When the Holy Spirit pours out in our heart a sense of the love of God, it involves our feelings in a very deep way. But it is also a grasp of some facts about Jesus and his death upon the cross. This is the relationship between Romans 5:5, and Romans 5:6–10. The love of God is directly experienced, it floods our hearts. But it is a feeling that has definite content to it. It is not just a matter of a burning sensation or a desire to dance or floods of tears – although any of those things might happen. Verses 6 to 10 explain the content of verse 5. It begins with 'For' or 'Because'. The reason why the experience of the love of God can be given is that the love of God is there. It is a fact of history. God has loved us. When the love of God is poured out in our hearts what is happening is that we are gripped by the sheer fact that though we are such sinners Jesus has died for us.

So Romans 5:6–8 describes the love of God. *For when we were still weak, at the right time Christ died for the ungodly* (5:6). *For one will scarcely die even for an upright person – although perhaps for a good person someone would dare even to die* (5:7). *But God commended his love towards us in that while we were yet sinners Christ died for us* (5:8).

He points to the need of God's love.

We were 'weak', 'ungodly', neither 'upright' nor 'good'. His love came entirely from him. We did nothing to deserve it at all. And it was not Jesus who took the first step. It was God the Father who took the first step of love. 'God so loved that he gave . . . ' (see John 3:16). Jesus says, I am not praying that the Father will love you! I do not need to. 'The Father himself loves you' (John 16:27).

How much we needed the Father's love. We were 'weak', unable to understand, unable to please God, without any inclination in us to obey the God of the Bible. We were 'ungodly', unlike God, with no sensitivity to God, without any love for God. We were not 'upright' and we were not 'good'. In verse 7 Paul is drawing a distinction between a person who is 'upright' and a person who is 'good'. 'For one will scarcely die even for an upright person – although perhaps for a good person someone would dare even to die.' There are some people who can be described as 'upright' and yet you do not exactly feel they are 'good'. The Pharisees presented themselves as 'upright' and in certain ways we could accept that they were so. They were moral, to all external appearances. Yet no one would want to die for a Pharisee! A 'good' person is more than just upright. He or she has warmth and love. You could, in rare circumstances, imagine it being possible that someone would lay down their life for a loving, tender, 'good' person.

But by nature we are neither! We were not by nature truly 'upright'; to God's viewpoint nor were the Pharisees.

We were not 'good'. We were without that true warmth of love and affection and generosity that comes from God. And yet God sent Jesus to die for us.

And we are described as 'sinners'. We had missed the will of God for us. We were out of accord with what he wanted us to be. We had offended him by the things we did, things we thought, things we imagined, things we left undone. But 'while we were yet sinners, Christ died for us'.

Paul points to the timing of God's love.

It was 'at the right time' that Christ died for the ungodly. This refers to the timing within the course of human history. Jesus was sent 'in the fullness of the times' (Gal. 4:4). He died at a planned time, and a time that was perfectly in the Father's will. God had prepared the world. The Jews had scattered throughout the Mediterranean world and had taken the Greek Old Testament with them. The Romans had built their roads for soldiers to travel on – but preachers used them too. The Greeks had taken their language throughout the cities of the Mediterranean world. The Romans had conquered the Mediterranean world and so there were few borders to cross when preachers travelled. It was the fullness of the times.

All attempts at salvation had failed. It was a time when philosophy had failed, when the early civilizations had risen and fallen, early science had failed, law and government and administration had failed, military conquerors had failed. It was a time when religion had failed, and even true religion had failed. For God had issued his law to Israel and had given them revelations of his will. But an intellectual knowledge of the truth will fail as much as anything else. When all was sin and shame, Jesus died for the ungodly.

These are the things that the Holy Spirit presses upon us when the love of God is poured out in the heart. The Holy Spirit pours into the heart a sense of God's love for us. The Spirit lets us see that although we have failed so awfully, sinned so badly, taken such a long time to learn the Father's will, the Father loves us.

The phrase 'the love of God' refers to God's love for us. Yet it is also true that when God's love for us is poured out in our hearts this way, we find ourselves truly loving God. We love him because he first loved us. And we find our hearts full of love for others. For the first time we are able to love everyone everywhere.

44

The Proof of Love (Romans 5:5–8)

God loves us! It is this that we see and feel when the love of God is poured out. It grips the heart. It is this that Jesus presses upon us when he 'baptizes' us, flooding our lives with the Holy Spirit. It is this that the Holy Spirit presses upon us in our daily experience when the 'love of God is being poured out in our hearts'.

Paul points to the proof of God's love.

'Christ died for the ungodly . . . God commended his love towards us in that while we were yet sinners Christ died for us.' God is recommending himself! He is holding himself up for our consideration and saying to us, 'Can you not see how much I love you? Why are you so fearful, so troubled, so sceptical?'

Jesus knew what he was doing. He set his face to go to Jerusalem. He wanted to avoid it if there was any other way. He said, Father, if there is any other way than this way, let me go the other way! But as he was praying he knew there was no other way and said, 'Nevertheless, not my will but your will be done!' He loved us that much. He knew the pain that was coming. He knew he would be a 'ransom' for sins. He told his disciples that he would suffer many things. He knew to a large extent what was happening.

God was showing you love when he sent Jesus. You do not need anything to recommend yourself to him. He is recommending himself to you. When Jesus died God was viewing you as a sinner and as nothing better than a sinner. You do not need to improve yourself for God to accept you. He knew the worst thing about you. He knew the worst thing you would ever do, and he sent Jesus to die for you despite what he knew. Jesus gave himself for our sins. Don't try to pretend you do not need him as a Saviour of sinners. You had best put yourself in the category of sinner! And then put him in the category of great and mighty Saviour! God knew what he was doing when he let Jesus hang upon that cross. God turned away from Jesus and let him cry, 'My God, my God, why have you forsaken me?' God had indeed for the moment forsaken Jesus and let him bear the sins of the entire human race. The Father himself was loving you. He abandoned his wonderful Son, the one who loved to feed the hungry and heal the sick, the one who tenderly taught his disciples, endured his enemies, encouraged the worst kind of sinner.

And the cross itself was despicable, disgusting, vile. There was nothing glamorous about it. But it was God's way of putting away our sins. See your sins laid on Jesus. Know that God does not need to hold anything against you. Your worst sins have been compensated for by the blood of Jesus. That blood will free you of guilt, cleanse your conscience. That blood will break the power of sin. That blood will prevail so as to get you to glory, if you but cast yourself on God's mercy in Jesus.

It is these things that are 'poured out' in our hearts by the Holy Spirit. You may ask, 'How can we know this outpouring of the love of God?' Really, no Christian should ever need to ask that question. Are you a Christian? Then do you need to ask that question? Do you not already know the love of God poured out in your heart? This is something that ordinarily should be experienced by us from the very earliest days of our being a Christian. It should not be a question of 'How can I know this?' If you are a Christian, why do you not know it already? But sometimes there can be a delay. It may be that you have never really seen the gospel, or never really submitted your life to Jesus. This holds back the experience of the love of God. Perhaps I can help you.

1. Begin by trusting in the blood of Jesus Christ. Believe the Father's love. Believe Jesus died for you. He died for the world, and the world includes you. To even wicked people Jesus said, 'My Father is giving you the true bread from heaven' (John 6:33). When the Spirit pours out the love of God in our hearts, he is simply 'sealing' to us what we have believed. You start by believing in God's love for you. Believe the blood of Jesus was shed so that you could be forgiven.

2. Are you grieving the Spirit? The flow of the love of God in your heart will be blocked by grieving the Spirit. The Spirit is a sensitive guest in our lives.

3. Has God turned his face away from you, withdrawn his presence? He can do that. But it will not last for ever.

If he is rebuking you because of some sin, deal with it. Put it away. If he is simply depriving you of his presence for a little while, it is to get you to value it more highly.

4. Live by the promise of John 7:37–39. 'If any person is thirsty let him come to me and drink . . . Out of his innermost being shall flow rivers of living water'. Notice two things there: 'come . . . drink'. You need to drink and go on drinking all your life. Drink of Jesus! Feed on him. Spend time with him. Don't get agitated looking self-consciously for an 'experience'. Just get on with believing. Maybe dramatically, maybe slowly with you scarcely noticing, the love of God will be poured out in your heart. Then keep your heart soft and tender. Keep yourself in the love of God.

45

Considering God's Love (Romans 5:8)

We are invited by Paul to consider the way God loved us. The love of God poured out in our hearts is a wonderful awareness that God is utterly and totally genuine in telling us how much he wants us. Amongst other things the Spirit shows us that the sacrifice of Jesus is God's recommendation of himself. 'God commended his love towards us'.

What do you do with a recommendation? You consider it. The cross is God's self-commendation. Consider the fact of God's love.

First: think of the way Jesus lived with his knowledge of the cross.

During all of his ministry, Jesus knew that he was to be the sacrifice for sin. He knew that in some unique way he was the Son of God. From his earliest days he had called God 'My Father' (see Luke 2:49). When he was about thirty years old he was anointed by the Holy Spirit and was immediately called to be the 'suffering servant' of the book of Isaiah. At his baptism, God's voice from heaven said, 'You are my beloved Son' – telling Jesus again who he was. The voice continued, '. . . in whom I am well pleased' –

telling Jesus that he was the Messiah of Isaiah 42:1, the one who was to die, according to Isaiah 53. Jesus began his ministry knowing that he was to die as a sacrifice for the sins of the world.

This is the love of Jesus for you, and the love of God the Father. For Jesus says, 'He who has seen me has seen the Father.' No one can ever look at God directly (see John 1:18) but God's Son reveals the Father to us. If you want to know how God feels about you, look at Jesus, the exposition of the Father's love.

Imagine what it is like being called to a certain work of ministry for God, and from the very first day knowing that God is calling you to suffer in the most intense way. That is the way it was for Jesus. He wanted to get it over and done with. He would say, 'I know that I am going to be plunged into terrible suffering and I am distressed until I get through it' (see Luke 12:50). Jesus knew – and the Father was experiencing it through his Son – that he was being invited to suffer intensely and agonizingly. But he was willing to go through it all because it was necessary for you and for me to be saved and to be reconciled to our heavenly Father.

When he told his disciples he would be a 'ransom' for sinners (Matt. 20:28) he knew he was to be a sacrifice. And he knew all about sacrifices. He knew what a 'sin offering' was. He knew how the animal was killed, how it was taken outside the camp and offered up for the sins of the people. Such treatment was given to animals day by day in the temple in Jerusalem, and any Jewish schoolboy could have told you about it. Jesus grew up with that knowledge. But during his ministry he had to face the fact that God's sacrifice for the sins of the world was not to be an animal's death. He was to be the sacrifice himself. Jesus had to live with this knowledge. His very baptism was a picture of it. His immersion into the waters of the river Jordan was his commissioning to be immersed into the agonies and sufferings of his death upon the cross.

Second: think of the disgrace of the cross.

Men and women are proud creatures. We like to be thought well of. We avoid disgrace. When for example a person is poor what hurts him or her more than the poverty is the sense of shame that it brings. Our reputation means a lot to us. We want others to feel that we are doing well. But think of the shame of the cross. Jesus was a failure in the eyes of the public. His friends came to the conclusion that he was a monumental failure. A couple of days after the death of Jesus, they were saying, 'We had hoped he was the one who was to redeem Israel.' He was shamed before his mother. He was stripped naked and hung up in public. It was this that he knew was coming during his ministry.

But this was the Father's will, and it was the way for the world to be saved. Jesus so loved the Father's will he would do anything for his heavenly Father. The Father so loved the world that he was willing to put his Son through the cross. This is the Father's self-commendation. This is God's way of saying: if you want to see how much I wanted you, look at what I did to get you. If you want to see how much

I wanted the enmity between you and me to come to an end, look at what I did to get that enmity to come to an end. If I had to punish sin, I wanted you so much that I found a way of punishing my Son for your sins so that I could get you to be my people and my friends. At the same time death could not hold my Son, so I got my Son back as well. But he had to go through being a sacrifice for sins. I chose to put him through it in order that I might get hold of you. Why do you doubt whether I love you? I am recommending my love to you in this way.

It is this knowledge that is poured out and pressed upon our hearts when the love of God is shed abroad by the Holy Spirit within us.

46

Love for Sinners (Romans 5:8)

'God commended his love. . . .' Paul does not want us to have the slightest doubt of the love of God for every one of us. The proof of God's love is the cross. The man Jesus suffered intensely. He was willing to suffer because of his love of the Father's will, and love for those who would believe on him and so become the Father's people.

Third: consider the people Jesus died for.

He died for everyone, for 'the many' (Rom. 5:15,19). But think of those who were around Jesus at the time he died for the human race. Think of the disciples. They all fled when Jesus was in trouble at the time of his arrest and condemnation by the authorities. Yet though they deserted Jesus, Jesus did not desert them. Though they fled from their task of serving him, he did not flee from his task of going to the cross to die for the very ones who had just abandoned him. He was commending his love. Even though he knew that these disciples of his were just about to shamefully forsake him and reveal how untrustworthy they were, still Jesus went on loving them.

Think of Peter. A few hours before Jesus was arrested

Jesus warned Peter that he was about to be severely tested and would deny Jesus. Peter said, 'No, Lord, I will never deny you.' Jesus said, 'Yes, you will. Before the cock crows twice, you will deny me three times.' But Peter would not accept it. 'I'll never deny you,' he said. A few hours later, Peter is in the courtyard where Jesus is going through a late-night investigation in a hurriedly gathered meeting at the house of the high priest. After a few questions from a servant girl Peter uses foul and ugly language and utterly denies that he has ever had anything to do with Jesus. This is the kind of person Jesus died for! Have you ever denied Jesus? Have you ever used foul and ugly language? How do you feel when someone treats you this way?

You see the love of God when you see how Jesus treated Peter. He did not reject Peter. Jesus knew what was going to happen. He told Peter, 'I have prayed for you.' Jesus had such love for Peter. Peter's denial only made Jesus pray for him. He went to the cross a few hours later. Peter is one of the ones for whom Jesus is dying.

This is the way God feels. God commends his love through the cross of Jesus. He does not reject us because of our failure; instead he has appointed his Son to die for us, and to pray for those who have believed. Peter was loved. God loved even the cursing, renegade disciples, the foul-mouthed denier of his Son. He loves us the same way.

Even more moving is the case of Judas. Personally, I do not think Judas was ever a believer. And if you could have got him to be honest, he would have told you he was not a believer. He knew he did not believe. Jesus knew from the beginning that Judas was a betrayer. He said on one occasion, 'You are all clean except one of you,' and on another occasion, 'one of you is a devil' (John 6:70). He said, 'Those you gave to me I have kept. However there is the case of Judas. . . .' He was called a 'person worthy of perdition' (John 17:12).

But God commended his love to Judas in that while Judas was a sinner Christ died for him! What love Jesus showed to Judas even while Judas was in the very act of betraying Jesus. Jesus never exposed Judas. His warning, 'One of you will betray me,' actually gave Judas a chance to back out of what he was planning and to cast himself on the mercy of Jesus. When Judas refused the opportunity, still Jesus did not publicly expose him. Jesus did not say which one it was who would be the betrayer. At the meal on the day before he was crucified, Jesus dipped a morsel of food into the soup and gave it to Judas, which seems to have been a special token of love and favour (John 13:26). It was an act of kindness and special attention. God was commending his love to Judas in that while Judas was in the midst of his sins, Christ was about to die for him.

But if God commended his love to Judas, he commends his love to us as well. He does not reject us, does not shut off the opportunity of salvation. Even though we have been an unbeliever in the midst of his people he still will not reject us. The love of Jesus – and the love of God through Jesus – is utterly unlike our love for anyone. It is surprising that he should love us at all. He pays the price for our sins before we were born, before we ever knew of him, before we had taken one step towards him.

We do not love like this at all. Our love is selfish. Even

when we are at our most affectionate and loving towards others there are often dubious and selfish reasons for even the best of our love. Pure unselfish generous self-giving love is almost unknown to us.

But this is the way the Father is towards us. He commends his love. He seeks to persuade us that he loves us and points us to the cross. When the love of God is poured out in our hearts by the Spirit we see it and believe and rejoice with a sense of how great and free is his grace towards us.

47

Love Despite Injustice (Romans 5:8)

Fourth: consider the injustice which Jesus went through.

We are all very sensitive to injustice, when it concerns ourselves. There are few things so embittering as to receive treatment which is unfair. It infuriates and enrages. Yet Jesus endured perverted justice and stayed calm amidst the terrible unfairness he went through. He would make only mild protests. He would say, 'Day after day I sat in the temple teaching and you did not arrest me. What you are doing now is just because you are fulfilling the power of evil forces' (see Luke 22:53). Or he would say, 'If I have spoken wrongly, bear witness to the wrong' (John 18:23). But his protests were calm and without denunciation.

He went through at least five trials. First of all, late at night he was taken to the home of Annas, father-in-law of Caiaphas the high priest, and subjected to what seems to have been an illegal night-time trial (John 18:13–24). There he got his first taste of the physical violence he was about to receive from Jewish and Roman officials (John 18:22). Then he was sent off to Caiaphas (John 18:24).

The next morning he went through his second trial, and the chief priests and elders of the people held discussions about how to get rid of him altogether by sentencing him to death (Matt. 27:1,2). There was no question of any real charge. Jesus had never been a political agitator. There would have to be some trumped-up charge if they were to get him judicially murdered. Then there came his third trial. He was sent off to Pilate (Luke 23:1; John 18:29) and there was accused, 'We found this fellow perverting our nation, and forbidding us to give tribute to Caesar, and saying that he himself is the Messiah, a king' (Luke 23:2). They were grasping at anything they could say to get him executed. 'He stirs up the people,' they said (Luke 23:5).

Pilate discovered that Jesus had Galilean connections, and so he had a good pretext to send Jesus to Herod (Luke 23:6–12). Jesus was put through a fourth trial, with the Jewish authorities vigorously accusing him. Herod wanted a few specially laid-on miracles, but could not get anything he wanted from Jesus. So Jesus was treated with contempt and mocked (Luke 23:11,12).

So back Jesus went to his fifth accusation, this time before Pilate again. There Jesus experienced the greatest injustice of all. He had previously been declared innocent (John 18:34, 'I find no fault in this man') and was again found innocent (Luke 23:15, 'nothing deserving death has been done by him'). But a battle of wills between Pilate and the Jews then began to take place, with the leaders inciting the people. Pilate's wife told of a revelation she had had that Jesus was innocent. The crowds screamed for his blood. Jesus was beaten up and ridiculed and spat upon. They dressed him up as a king and mocked him. All this at a trial! Finally, because a riot was rapidly approaching, Pilate handed him over to be crucified, making feeble attempts to wash his hands of responsibility. As if a little bowl of water could atone for such a monumental injustice.

What was it that brought God the Father to allow his Son to go through such agonies? It was love. 'God commended his love towards us in that while we were sinners Christ died for us.'

Who crucified Jesus? You could say it was Caiaphas or the Jewish parliament. You could say it was the people who screamed, 'Crucify him'. Peter said, 'You handed over Jesus to be killed' (see Acts 3:12–15). You could say it was Judas, the betrayer (see Mark 14:21). You could say it was Pilate who tried to shrug off responsibility and to do what was right, but eventually committed a great perversion of his responsibility.

But we can go deeper. It was our sins that sent Jesus to the cross. You could say Jesus crucified himself! Judas delivered him up (Matt. 26:14–16); the priests delivered him up (Matt. 27:18); Pilate delivered him up (Matt. 27:26). But the deeper truth is 'The Son of God loved me and gave himself over for me.' And back behind the love of the Son was the love of the Father. The Son of Man was lifted up on the cross because God so loved the world that he gave up his Son (see John 3:15,16). The Father's plan was to rescue the world from sin. Only Jesus his Son could do it. And the Father demonstrated his love in handing his Son over to the cross.

Jesus was willing to go through all of this. He had some idea that it was coming. He had warned his disciples that he must suffer many things at the hands of the leaders of

Israel. He knew all about the betrayer and had known from the very beginning. He knew what the Jewish leaders would do to him.

This is where you see love. You see it in Jesus' surrender of all his natural desires, in his willingness to go through pain and shame and ridicule. In the midst of all these sufferings Jesus was dying for the very people that were treating him in this way. How resentful we get at the slightest injustice. But Jesus knew it was needful, and was demonstrating the Father's love.

48

Love in Gethsemane (Romans 5:8)

Fifth: consider the agony of Gethsemane.

This was the one time in the life of Jesus where he did not want to do the Father's will. Generally he said, 'My food is to do the will of the one who sent me' (John 4:33). But on this particular occasion he drew back for a while from doing the Father's will. He knew that his death would be very soon. He knew the precise way he would die – by crucifixion. He knew the precise time it would be – at Passover (Matt. 26:1,2). He knew that within a matter of hours he would be dead and buried (Matt. 26:12). He invited three of his closest disciples to pray with him, but they fell asleep again and again, and did not realize the greatness of the crisis that was coming.

So Jesus prayed alone amidst sleepy disciples. He was in an agony. He threw himself to the ground (Luke 22:41) and began to ask that he might be relieved of the terrible thing that faced him. Father, if there is any way of saving the world other than going to be crucified, please let me do it some other way. I do not know whether another way is possible, but if it is possible please take this cup of suffering away from me (see Luke 22:42a). He offered loud cries and prayers with tears to God who in one way or another could save him (Heb. 5:7).

He prayed alone. There was not a single other human being in the world who would know what he was talking about if he tried to share what was happening. His closest colleagues had been told again and again but they were a few yards away fast asleep! Is there any loneliness like this? This was the very thing for which the Son of God had come into the world. But he got no help.

He prayed to be released. Is there another way for sins to be paid for? But as he prayed he saw that there was no other way. So he went a step further in his praying. 'Nevertheless not my will but your will be done!' This is not the kind of 'If it be thy will' praying that we often hear. It is not, 'I have no idea what you are going to do, but whatever it is you can do it.' No. At this point Jesus does know the Father's will. At this point he knows that there is no other way. The crucifixion and everything that is going to come with it is the way that he must go. So he gives himself over to the Father's will. 'Your will – and I can see what it is – be done!'

Has there ever been love like this? Here is a human being, facing the possibility of having to go voluntarily and willingly to crucifixion, the most painful and shameful mode of execution the ancient world could think of, a mode of execution that was not allowed for any Roman citizen because it was so disgusting and degrading that the Romans would not allow their worst criminals to suffer it without stripping them of their citizenship first.

And one must remember that Jesus was a human being!

It would be a great mistake to say, 'Well, Jesus was the Son of God, so for him it was alright. He would be able to bear it!' Not at all! Jesus was a man. He felt the pain of those nails in precisely the same way that you would feel it if a nail were smashed through your feet. He felt the shame of hanging naked in public in precisely the same way that you would feel the shame of hanging naked in public.

And the dread of what was coming affected him in Gethsemane in precisely the same way that it would have affected you. What would you do if you knew crucifixion was in store for you within a few hours? You would perhaps do what Jesus did. You would beg people to pray for you. You would get down on your knees. You would pray as you had never prayed before. You would plead with the Father to somehow release you from this trial. You would weep; you would pray with loud cries. You would perhaps throw yourself upon the ground. Jesus did all of this. He was a human being. Although he was God, the fact that he was God was not allowed to cancel his feelings as a human being. He knew that he was God, but his feelings were precisely the same kind of feelings that we would have had in that situation.

This is love! God so loved the world that he gave his Son to this kind of death. It was the only way. Sin was being paid for. Sin is so vile, so awful, so disgusting to a holy God, that this is what sin does. The price of sin was coming upon him. God was commending his love in that while we were yet sinners, Christ set his face deliberately to go to the cross, and said, out of love for us, 'Your will be done'.

49

Jesus Abandoned (Romans 5:8)

Sixth: consider Jesus' cry concerning his being deserted by the Father.

Here is perhaps the greatest and deepest aspect of the love of God seen in the cross. Here, in a most wonderful way, 'God commended his love'. What is this cry? In Matthew's version (27:46) we have one of the few places where we have the exact words that Jesus used. In a mixture of Hebrew and Aramaic he called upon God. 'My God! My God!', he cried, remembering Psalm 22:1 in the Hebrew version which he knew. Then he used his own mother tongue and called out in Aramaic, 'Why have you forsaken me?'

It was not simply a cry of anger or loneliness. It was certainly not a cry of failure. What was happening was that at this point the sin of the world was placed upon Jesus and the Father turned his back on Jesus. This is a very mysterious subject. No one can really understand it. But Jesus for a while lost all sense of the presence of his Father.

For the first time ever, it seems, Jesus called his Father simply 'My God'. This is totally unique on the lips of Jesus. Every time we find Jesus praying we find him using the word 'Father', but now he had no joy in feeling and knowing the companionship of his Father. It was this that he was dreading in the Garden of Gethsemane. He knew a few hours earlier that he would have to experience the holy anger of God against sin. He knew that sin separates from God and that he himself was going to be treated as a sacrifice, with the holy fire of God's anger against sin coming down on him.

There was darkness all around him. It was a purely miraculous darkness. It was not an eclipse; it is not possible to have a total eclipse at Passover time. The very creation was frowning upon Jesus. His disciples had abandoned him. His closest friends could not help him. Now God himself switched off the lights of the universe and abandoned him, in some mysterious way. At this precise point Jesus became a 'ransom for many' (Mark 10:45). All his life Jesus had been 'in the heart of the Father' (John 1:18). Until this point he had been able to say, 'My Father is with me' (John 16:32). Now he experienced what it is to be forsaken by God. Jesus had deliberately walked to the cross, deliberately taken a step which would lead to his coming under the judgment of God. This is love! Here is the Father commending his love. Here is Jesus showing us how far he is willing to go to get hold of those who will believe in him as Saviour and Lord.

This cry of abandonment contains a question. 'Why have you forsaken me?' This means that there was more in the cross than even Jesus expected. We know that Jesus knew he would be crucified. He has told his disciples only a few hours ago that he would be crucified. Yet here he is asking a question. There was a depth of abandonment that took him by surprise. He was not expecting abandonment to the depth that he was experiencing it. It seems that for the first time ever – without any sin on his part – he did not understand what was happening. So he asks an agonized question. 'What has happened?', he asks. 'Why have you forsaken me?'

Although this is a very mysterious matter and we must be reverently cautious as we look at such an amazing thing, to some extent we can see how something like this had to happen. There have been many believers who have felt utterly abandoned by God. How would Jesus ever be able to sympathize with our sense of abandonment if Jesus himself had never felt any sense of abandonment by God? One aspect of sin is total bewilderment, loss of clarity of mind, God forsakenness. So great was the Father's love towards the human race that he put his Son even through this awful experience. Nothing is more terrible than to feel yourself forsaken and at enmity with God. Nothing is more frightening than to call upon God and not be heard. Jesus felt as if God himself were attacking him and casting him to hell. He was experiencing the full weight of the Father's anger against sin.

What incredible love is here. This is the Father commending his love. Here is Jesus showing us his love. Why should anyone ever doubt that the Father loves us? This is what is poured out upon us as the Holy Spirit baptizes us with the love of God. This is the pledge and proof that God is willing to forgive and heal and bless and restore the very worst of sinners. This is the proof that salvation is open to Peter, to Judas (if he will but believe), to Pilate, to Caiaphas. What loving kindness, what fatherly mercy! What a proof of God's boundless mercy! We can be sure that such love will continue. What encouragement there is to believe that this love will stay with me for ever. A God who loves like this, this is the kind of Saviour-God I can trust for ever.

50

Encouraging Logic (Romans 5:9–10)

We have seen two ways of knowing the love of God. One way is by logic. Paul makes deductions from the cross of Jesus. Another way of knowing the love of God is by direct experience.

The direct experience enables us to use the logic. When we know something of the love of God poured out in our hearts, we are able to make a few deductions in the way that Paul does in Romans 5:9–10

Look at his great logic: *Much more then, being now justified by his blood we shall be saved from wrath through him* (Rom. 5:9).

If we are justified, 'much more' shall we be kept saved. The important thing is to be justified, declared righteous by God himself by being covered with Jesus' righteousness. By the blood of Jesus Christ, sin has been dealt with. Its punishment has been borne.

So we shall be safe in judgment day. The 'wrath of God' will be poured out on all sin in the day of wrath, when Jesus comes to deal righteously with sin. Only one thing can keep us safe and that is the blood of Jesus which enabled us to be justified.

God has done the more difficult thing, which is to get a sinner justified in the first place. Now that that has been done the rest is easy! If we have been saved by Jesus' blood (the hardest part), we shall certainly be saved from the wrath of God in judgment day (which is easier).

The difficult thing was to find a way of salvation, a way of justifying us in the first place. Sin is so great and terrible a thing that it was a problem even for God himself! God cannot just ignore sin. God does not just say, 'Forget it. We'll pretend it did not happen.' God is holy. He does not shut his eyes to sin. He sees things the way they are. So for a person ever to be justified before God is an incredible thing. But God has done it. By means of the blood of Jesus, we can be freed from guilt altogether and declared right- eous, because we are in Christ and in his righteousness.

We shall be kept safe. In a sense you could say we have been through judgment day already! With regard to our position as righteous people in Christ, everything has already been decided. Judgment day has already been dealt with in that respect. I shall never be condemned. Judgment day will allocate rewards and reveal the way everyone has lived and sort out all controversies. Being now justified is the most difficult and incredible thing of all. Much more then – being now justified by his blood – I shall be saved from wrath through Jesus.

Verse 10 explains further. *For if when we were enemies, we were reconciled to God by the death of his Son, much more being reconciled shall we be saved by being joined on to his life.*

Once again it is a highly logical statement. It argues from the bigger thing to the smaller thing. The biggest thing God had to do was to overcome the enmity between us and God. It was a two-way enmity. Not only did we show enmity towards God. More serious, God showed enmity towards us. Although he loved us, yet he hated sin. He loved us and hated us at the same time. It was not easy for God to find a way to be reconciled to us. God has to find a way to be pacified when he sees us, as well as finding a way for us to be reconciled to him. When the Scripture says God 'reconciled' us, it means that he removed the obstacle of his wrath towards our sins.

But God found a way, 'through the death of his Son'. The anger of God against sin fell on Jesus, so that it did not need to fall on us.

Once again Paul uses his 'much more' argument. If God has done the big thing, 'how much more' will he do the relatively easy thing. When we were the objects of God's anger, God found a way of dealing with the problem. We were reconciled to God by the death of his Son. So now the rest is straightforward. 'Much more being reconciled, we shall be saved by being joined on to his life.' The particular way in which God will bring us through to final salvation is through the fact that we have been joined on to Jesus. We not only get forgiven, we get united to Jesus, joined on to his life. We died in Christ, we were buried in Christ, and then we were united to Christ in his resurrec- tion. He ever lives to make intercession for us. He is praying that we shall get to be where he is in glory. He prays with perfect faith, and he gets his prayers answered. He does not pray for everyone in this way; John 17:9 tells us that. He died for the world (John 3:16) but he prays for those who believe (John 17:9). He offers us salvation; we need to be justified. After we know we are justified we know we are the ones Jesus is praying for. He is able to keep us from falling. He is able to restore us. The devil has been cast down and removed from his position of power. We ourselves have been transferred into the kingdom of God's grace.

We still are in the little sub-paragraph that deals with the outpoured love of God. This too is part of what we are assured of as the love of God is poured out in our hearts. The Spirit shows us how much God loves us. The big thing was to have been reconciled to God in the first place. Now 'how much more shall we be saved in his life'.

51

Enjoying God (Romans 5:11)

One might think that the outpoured love of God is so great a blessing that there is nothing that could be added to it. But Paul does have one more thing to say as he brings this paragraph (5:1–11) to a close. Paul says, *And not only so . . .* There is one step higher even than the outpoured love of God. What is even higher than knowing God's outpoured love is that we go on to rejoice in God himself.

It is as though we are exploring a mighty river and are following it upstream to discover its source. God pours out his love in our hearts. God enables us to feel and see with the clarity of the Spirit that he has commended his love to us. But as we follow this love upstream to its source we come to God himself. 'God so loved that he gave. . . .' God's actions in the past. God's actions in our present experience. God's promises concerning the future. God! We glory in God himself.

What makes it possible for us to rejoice in this way is that we know that right now we are reconciled to him. Paul says, *And not only so, but we also rejoice in God through our Lord Jesus Christ, through whom we have now received the reconciliation* (Rom. 5:11). We are justified! God's displeasure towards us is gone. Our fears and dislike of the God of the Bible are gone. Our guilt and our guilt feelings are gone. The remnants of sinfulness make no difference. We walk in the light and the blood of Jesus goes on cleansing us from all sin. Our consciences are sprinkled clean so that we are able to serve God as the living God. So we are thrilled with God himself. 'My soul shall make its boast in the LORD' (Ps. 34:2). 'O magnify the Lord with me, and let us exalt his name together' (Ps. 34:3). 'I will rejoice in the LORD, I will be joyful in the God of my salvation' (Hab. 3:18). 'God my exceeding joy' (Ps. 43:4).

It is all through Jesus. Paul loves to mention the name of Jesus. There are times when he seems to be mentioning the name as often as he can, and savouring it every time he does so. 'The Lord Jesus Christ.' How often he has been mentioning the name. 'Peace . . . through our Lord Jesus Christ . . . Christ died for the ungodly . . . Christ died for us . . . Reconciled by the death of his Son . . . We rejoice through our Lord Jesus Christ.' I once asked an ex-member of a heretical sect who had come to know Jesus and had left his cult, 'What was it that led you to Jesus and to salvation?' He said, 'I was reading the New Testament and as I read I could not help noticing that the New Testament made so much more of Jesus than any of the talks I heard in our meetings.' That is it! Jesus is everywhere in the pages of the New Testament. Jesus! Jesus! How sweet is his name.

Jesus has brought us to God. He is now our friend. The Creator of the universe has loved me. He took the initiative. I did not love him. He loved me. I can think of no reasons why he should love me, although I can think of lots of reasons why he shouldn't love me. But he did. He set his heart on me. So we rejoice in God himself. We love him just the way he is. We rejoice in his power. Nothing is too hard for him. We enjoy his surprises. He is the living God. We like his presence. We know he fills the universe with his presence and yet he is right here now with me. We rejoice in his faithfulness, his constancy. We enjoy knowing that he knows everything. He knows how many grains of sand there are on a thousand seashores.

We enjoy his wisdom. He has never made a mistake. Though we have been upset with him he has always proved true. He has been faithful in protecting us, faithful in keeping his promises. We rejoice in his love, his mercy, his grace, his compassion, his patience with us, his goodness in loving the righteous and the unrighteous. We love and rejoice in his holiness even though it makes us a little nervous. Yet we rejoice to know he is pure. We would not have him any other way. We are glad that he wants us so much that he can get jealous if he does not have us. We love his nearness to us, his greatness above us. We love his beauty, the beauty of his holiness and the beauty of his happiness. We love his glory, when everything within him shines out.

Best of all we know that such a God is our Friend. A Friend who knows the worst thing about us, but tells us he will never reject us. A Friend who has plans for us, but will never moralize us. A Friend who is powerful. A Friend who is affectionate. A Friend who accepts us. A Friend who will not expose us.

And so we rejoice. We rejoice with full hearts. We rejoice with our voice. We say, 'Sing praises to God, sing praises! Sing praises to our King, sing praises!' (Ps. 47:6).

We rejoice with our bodies. There are times when we are together with God's people when we want to clap (Ps. 47:1). David got so joyful he started dancing, to the dismay of his wife (2 Sam. 6:14). We rejoice with our friends. We rejoice with ourselves. There are times when we are walk- ing down the road and someone smiles at us. We wonder, 'Does that person know me? Why is he smiling?' Then we realize. We were smiling at him! God was the joy of our countenance. We have received our reconciliation!

52

An Unfinished Comparison
(Romans 5:12)

Romans 5:12 introduces a new subsection in the flow of
the letter. In the previous verses Paul has been telling us
about the immediate results of being justified by faith. We
have peace with God (5:1), access into God's grace (5:2a),
an expectation of glory (5:2b), an understanding of our
troubles (5:3,4), an experience of the love of God (5:5–10)
and joy because now in the immediate present we are
enjoying reconciliation with God (5:11).

But actually we receive not only these particular blessings
but also something greater and deeper. Our entire position
is changed. Romans 5:12–21 goes on to tell us how being
justified and having access into God's grace and being
immediately reconciled to God is part of something even
greater. We used to be 'in Adam', but now we are 'in
Christ', and the grace of God rules over us.

It seems difficult at first to follow the complicated
argument of verses 12–21. But once we see its structure
and the way the argument moves it is not so hard. The
key is to realize that Paul starts a comparison but does not
finish it at first. He starts off like this: *Therefore, just as
through one man sin entered into the world, and through sin death
came, and in this way death spread to all people, because all people*

sinned . . . (Rom. 5:12). The opening word, *Therefore*, introduces a new subsection. It is as though Paul were saying, 'The position then is this'. And he goes on to tell us about something that is both a conclusion to everything he has said in Chapters 1:18 to 5:11, but also prepares the way for everything he is going to say in Chapters 6–8. When Paul started, he was thinking of saying something like:

Just as sin entered into the world, and through sin death came, and in this way death spread to all people, because all people sinned . . .	*so in the same way* righteousness came into the world . . .'

He was intending to make some comparison like this, and he does get to that comparison in verse 18. But as Paul is making this 'Just as . . . so' comparison, he feels he ought to digress to make two things clear before he finishes his comparison. So he turns aside to deal with two points, and then he comes back to finish what he was going to say. The thread of the argument goes like this.

Verse 12 An unfinished comparison
Therefore, just as through one man sin entered into the world, and through sin death came, and in this way death spread to all people, because all people sinned. . . .

Verses 13–14. A digression to explain something
For until the law sin was in the world but sin is not imputed where there is no law (v.13). But death reigned from Adam until Moses, even over those whose sins were not like the

transgression of Adam, who is a pattern of the One who is to come (v.14).

Verses 15–17. Another digression to explain a further point

But the gift is not like the trespass. For if the many died by the trespass of the one man, how much more did the grace of God and the free gift that came through the grace of that one man Jesus Christ abound for the many (v.15). And the gift is not like what happened through the one man who sinned. For, on the one hand, the judgment came from one sin, and brought condemnation, but, on the other hand, the free gift arose because of many trespasses and leads to justification (v.16). For if by the trespass of the one man death reigned through that one man, how much more will those who receive the abundance of grace and the gift of righteousness reign in life through the one person Jesus Christ (v.17)

Verses 18–19. The comparison is then completed

So then as through one man's trespass something happened for all people for their condemnation, so also through one man's righteous act something happened for all people for justification of life (v.18). For as through the disobedience of one man the many were constituted sinners, so also through the obedience of the one man the many will be constituted righteous (v.19).

In verses 20–21 a further point is made about the law, which we shall look at later. There are some things that we can learn from Paul's unfinished comparison.

First: there was a specific time in history when 'Sin entered into the world'.

We do not know the precise date. It was thousands of years before Jesus came. But there was a time in the calendar of the human story when humankind fell into sin. Paul does not explain the origin of sin. He does not even mention the devil, who led the human race into sin. He simply states the fact that sinfulness has come into the human race and it has a definite beginning. Genesis 3 records something that happened in history. True, the style of writing in Genesis 3 is partly parabolic; the snake is certainly a picture-language way of speaking of the devil. But it is a parabolic way of talking about something that actually happened in the story of the human race. The world as we find it is not the world as God made it. There was a time when 'sin entered into the world'. This is actually encouraging to us. If our world as we find it is not what God intended it to be, then there is hope that God will get it back on course. That is precisely what God is doing. Adam brought our world down: Jesus will restore it. Paul will show that God's grace is so much bigger than Adam's sin or our sin. He is expounding the 'much more' of Romans 5:9,10, and the phrase 'in his life' in Romans 5:10. Joined on to the life of our Lord Jesus Christ, we shall get back 'much more' than we lost through Adam.

53

Adam and Christ (Romans 5:12)

We have learned that there was a time in history when 'sin entered into the world'.

Second: sin and death entered the world through the one man Adam.

The story of the human race revolves first around Adam whose sin had world–wide consequences. *Therefore, just as through one man sin entered into the world, and through sin death came . . .*

Third: death came into the world through sin.

Paul says: *through sin death came, and in this way death spread to all people, because all people sinned . . .* God told Adam at the beginning, 'In the day you eat of it you will surely die.'
  What was this 'death'?

This death involved: a broken relationship with God.

Immediately after Adam sinned, his fellowship with God was lost. When God came seeking fellowship with Adam,

Adam was far from wanting fellowship with him. He was full of fear and wanted to hide himself from God. This is spiritual death, the opposite of the life that consists of knowing God (John 17:3). Adam excluded himself from God, and God excluded him from paradise.

This death involved: damaged relationships with people.

Before his sin Adam had been delighted with the gift of his wife (Gen 2:23). Immediately after his sin he blames her and says, 'The woman you gave me, she gave me some fruit' (Gen. 3:12). Damaged relationships were the mark of the world from that point onwards. The first brother in the Bible was the first murderer in the Bible.

This death involved: a damaged relationship with the world.

Immediately after his sin we learn of the damage that came to creation itself. Pain came into the world (Gen. 3:16), the ground became unproductive (Gen. 3:18), work became arduous (Gen. 3:1). Death was written into humankind's environment and relationships.

This death involved: physical decay and termination in physical death.

The most notable and conspicuous aspect of Adam's plight was physical decay, and its termination in physical death.

'Dust you are, and to dust you shall return' (Gen. 3:19). It was this death that spread to the entire human race through the first sin of humankind. 'The wages of sin is death.'

So far three things have emerged from Romans 5:12. There was a time in history when 'Sin entered into the world' (see Ch. 52). Sin and death entered the world through the one man Adam. Death came into the world through sin.

Fourth: all people sinned in Adam.

Everyone sinned in this one man, Adam. Paul says, *death spread to all people, because all people sinned* . . . This last phrase, 'because all people sinned', has been the subject of much debate. Some say it means that all die because they follow Adam's bad example and sin themselves (but in verses 13 to 14 Paul says that death reigned over those who did not follow Adam's example by transgressing a law). Others think it means that everyone dies because we inherit sinfulness from our ancestors and from Adam (but it does not say 'all were sinful'; it says 'all sinned', a definite single sin). Some think it means that we all sin personally in ourselves and so bring death upon ourselves (but this is not confirmed by the following verses).

The true interpretation is that all sinned 'in Adam'. As Paul continues in verses 15 to 19 it becomes clear that everyone sinned in the one sin of Adam. When he says that 'all sinned' and when he says there was one trespass of one man, he is speaking of the same event.

Adam represents us. He was one of us. We have the same human nature as he had. We are from one human race. God made 'from one, every nation of people' (Acts 17:26). So when Adam was on trial to test his obedience, I was also on trial to test my obedience. When Adam failed it was the proof that my human nature fails. He was representing the whole human race. When he sinned I sinned. Adam was one of us. We could not have had a better representative than Adam. What he did, we would have done. He was no stronger than us. If he was vulnerable to the devil, so would we have been.

The way in which we fell so calamitously is also the way in which the offer of restoration comes to us. When Jesus came to be our Saviour the method God chose was also the way of representation and substitution. Jesus died on the cross 'for us', in the same way that Adam was under test of obedience 'for us'. We get to be righteous in Jesus, just as we were sinners in Adam. Jesus was a second and last Adam. He is our perfect representative. He is truly man. When we put our faith in him we become 'in Christ'. Jesus was a second and last Adam, a true and perfect and sinless man. He did not descend from us, and we do not descend from him in any physical way. But when we take him as our Saviour, he then is joined on to us not only by way of representation, but also there comes into being a common life. We get to be 'in' him. Jesus reversed the fall. Adam had a common life with the entire human race. It was this common life that made Adam our perfect representative in Eden. Jesus follows the reverse order. First he became our representative and substitute, substituting for the entire human race. When we put our faith in him we get united with him and we then get bound up with his life. We become one flesh with him (Eph. 5:28–30). We have one spirit with him (1 Cor. 6:17). We are fused together with him (Rom. 6:5). We share his death, his burial, his resurrection, his life, his home in heaven, his destiny.

'In' Adam all die. He is our ultimate grandfather and represented us. But he failed. Jesus came as our representative. When we believe in him we become 'in Christ' in the deepest possible way. The blessings of Jesus flow down to us even more than the penalties and losses flowed to us from Adam.

54

After Adam, before Moses (Romans 5:13–14)

When Paul mentioned (5:12) that 'death spread to all people, because all people sinned', it obviously needed fuller explanation.

He says, in verses 13 and 14, *For until the law sin was in the world but sin is not imputed where there is no law* (5:13). *But death reigned from Adam until Moses, even over those whose sins were not like the transgression of Adam . . .* (5:14).

In the period between the time of Adam and Moses, the time before the law was given, there was plenty of sinning! 'Sin was in the world.'

We recall some sins that took place before the giving of the law: the murder of Abel (Gen. 4:8), the wickedness in the days of Noah (Gen. 6), the story of Sodom and Gomorrah (Gen. 19), the sins of Joseph's brothers and Potiphar's wife. Even in the chosen family of Abraham there was plenty of sin. Joseph's brothers wanted to kill him, and eventually sold him into slavery (Gen. 37:18, 25–27). Judah was guilty of immorality (Gen. 38). There was sin before the law.

But 'sin is not imputed where there is no law'. What does this mean? It does not mean that sin is not called sin. Even before the law God said to Cain, 'Sin is crouching at the door' (Gen. 4:7). Even before the law Joseph said, 'How could I do this great evil and sin against God?' (Gen. 39:9). So what does it mean, 'Sin is not imputed'?

Sin is there but it is not counted as a legal matter, liable to legal punishment. It is not reckoned as punishable, where there is no law.

It might be helpful if we put it like this. There are two types of sin. I could call one of them 'legally tolerated sin' and the other I could call 'legally forbidden sin'. I once knew of a certain place where two roads met. It was quite a dangerous junction. Cars used to come down a hill at a very dangerous speed. They used not to stop at the junction but each car would assume it had the right of way. People were sometimes killed. Those drivers were guilty of care-lessness. One could say they were guilty of sin. But there was no 'Stop' sign at the junction. There was no law about who had to stop. Drivers often were guilty of carelessness but their sin was of the 'legally tolerated' kind.

One day after a bad accident in which someone was killed, the authorities did something about it. It now was obligatory for all cars to stop before they passed over that junction. A signal was put there telling the cars to stop before crossing. Think of that road junction. Drivers sinned even before the 'law' was written up. Often they drove carelessly. They sometimes killed people. They were doing things they should not have been doing. But it was never 'counted' against them as a crime. They were never punished. There was no law that said they should be punished. They were guilty (often) but the sin could not be legally 'counted' or charged against them because they were not breaking any law. Their sin was 'legally tolerated'.

But think of the situation after the 'Stop' sign was placed at that junction, after the law was proclaimed that cars should stop. From that point on if any driver was careless and did not stop, he or she had broken a law! Their sin was not only sin, it was legally forbidden. They had transgressed an instruction that had been put clearly into writing.

This is Paul's point. Before the law of God was given on Mount Sinai through Moses, there was plenty of sin. And it was called sin! But the sins were not breaking a written law. They were not transgressions of something that had been clearly stated. Many sinned, before the law of Moses was given, and God was displeased with what they did. God rebuked Cain for his sin. But actually when Cain killed Abel the command, 'Thou shalt not kill' had not been issued! Cain had not broken a law explicitly. He was sinning against conscience, against the will of God, but not against written law. There was no written law.

So in Romans 5:13,14, the point is that Adam's sin was a transgression of an openly stated and explicit command. God issued a one-point law, 'You shall not eat of the tree of the knowledge of good and evil . . . In the day you eat of it you shall surely die.' Adam broke an explicit law when he sinned. But what about those after Adam and before Moses? After Adam, God gave no more explicit commands like the one he had given to Adam, and like the ones he would give through Moses. People sinned, but their sins were legally tolerated.

Yet people died! Why did they die? They had not broken a command to which a death penalty was attached. When

God said to Adam, 'In the day that you eat of it you shall surely die,' he was referring to breaking an openly stated law. But the people after Adam did not break any openly stated law. So why did they die? Some of them were children! Why should children die? (I am not saying Paul has only children in mind, but they are certainly included, for there were children who died between the days of Adam and Moses.)

The answer is that people died because they had sinned 'in Adam'. They shared Adam's punishment because they had shared Adam's sin. We were all there when Adam sinned. He was sinning for us as well as for himself.

This is Paul's way of proving what he said in Romans 5:12, 'death spread to all people, because all people sinned'. All people sinned in Adam. Adam sinned for me. I sinned 'in Adam'. He did what I would have done. He was my representative.

55

Adam as a Pattern (Romans 5:14)

Romans 5:14 speaks of 'Adam, who is a pattern of the One who is to come.' Adam was a pattern or a 'type' of Jesus. Here the word 'type' has a special meaning. It means 'pattern'. When you look at Adam you can see certain principles that apply again in the person of Jesus.

'Typology' is the name for the study of these 'patterns' in God's actions. Years ago Christians used to see a lot of typology in the Bible. Often people saw patterns in a way that was very fanciful, and the subject came into disrepute. Recently Christians have taken it seriously again.

Typology is not allegory. Allegory is spotting coincidences between things that may be quite different. Typology is interpreting by noticing that some events have principles in them that are repeated at a higher level. What makes for good typology is that the principles are really there. They do not have to be 'read in' to the text. The Passover contains principles (salvation by substitution, salvation by faith) which are repeated in the cross of Jesus. But the principles were there even before the cross of Jesus.

Typology is often badly done. When a favourite doctrine is read into odd details without any supporting evidence, typology is being badly used. For example, when the dimensions of the ark (2½ cubits by 3½ cubits) are

interpreted to mean, 'We only know Jesus partially' (because of the two halves!), we ask is there evidence anywhere in the Bible or the culture of the ancient world that
a half in a measurement stood for incompleteness? Is there
any principle which is being repeated in Jesus? Such an
interpretation is not true typology. It seems to be reading
into the Old Testament a nice idea which is taught
elsewhere by the Scripture, but is not in this text. Typology is not just an exercise of the imagination.

Typology is not the same as symbolism. The rainbow is
a symbol of God's mercy (Gen. 9:13–16) but it is not a
type.

Typology is not illustration. Marriage is an 'illustration'
of the relationship between the believer and Jesus. But
marriage is not a type. It is an illustration. A soldier in
armour is an illustration of spiritual weapons, but is not a
type. Typology always involves the repetition of principles
which were genuinely there in the type as well as in the
fulfilment.

But in Romans 5:14 you have true typology. Adam is a
type or pattern of Jesus Christ. One can see that certain
principles in the story of Adam are repeated at a higher level
in Jesus. This is what typology is. It is not simply noticing
accidental similarities, or reading into the Old Testament
text one's favourite doctrines. It is when there is a repetition
of principles. In the case of Adam one can see certain ways
of doing things that actually and literally applied then, but
which were repeated at a higher level in Jesus. We can pick
out six of them.

1. Adam was a real person.
2. Adam was a participant in the life of the human race.
3. Adam was appointed by God to represent the human race.
4. Adam did something which affected the destiny of the human race.
5. It was one crucial deed that affected the world's destiny.
6. Men and women follow up what Adam did by their own personal sins.

These six things are true in and of themselves. They are independently true, even before we come to consider what Jesus did. Even without considering Jesus these six things would be true. Good typology works this way. The principles that one sees in the type are true in and of themselves, even before one comes to see how they are repeated at a higher level.

See how these six matters are repeated at an altogether higher level in Jesus.

1. Jesus also was a real person, a historical person.
2. God appointed Jesus also to be the representative of the entire human race. (Notice that I change the order. In the case of Adam, sharing of life came before representation. In the case of Jesus, representation came before the sharing of life.)
3. As Adam drew the world to himself when he sinned, so when Jesus was bearing the sin of the world he was drawing the entire world to himself. This is the meaning of John: 'When I am lifted up [on the cross] I will draw all men unto myself' (John 12:32). This does not refer

to preaching. It refers to the historical fact that Jesus was 'tasting death for every person' (Heb. 2:9). If one person died for all people, said Paul, then the 'all' died! The entire world was put in a different position by the death of Jesus, just as the entire world was put into a different position by the sin of Adam.

4. As with Adam, it was one single event in the life of Jesus that was the crucial factor in what he did for the world, his act of obedience in going to the death of the cross.

5. As with Adam, the act of Jesus is open to ratification. When we believe we are ratifying, confirming, acknow-ledging what Jesus did. We follow up what Jesus did by our own personal commitment to him, just as men and women of the world (and we ourselves before our salvation) follow up the sin of Adam with their own sins.

6. Just as we were 'in Adam' we get to be 'in Christ' and to share in the resurrected life of Jesus. We get united with him in his resurrection. Our life is hidden with Christ in God. Just as the sinfulness of Adam flowed into us, so the life of Jesus flows into us as the sap of a tree into its branches. Adam is a pattern of the One who is to come.

56

Grace greater than Sin (Romans 5:15)

Paul is about to compare Adam and Christ. Yet he is still not quite ready to come to his comparison. He will get there in Romans 5:18. He does not want anyone to think that Adam and Jesus are equally influential in their impact upon the human race. There is a parallelism between what happens through Adam and through Jesus. Yet the two procedures have some contrasts as well. Paul says, *But the free gift is not like the trespass* (Rom. 5:15a). By 'free gift' he means the generous act of obedience of Christ on the cross, an act of obedience that brings us righteousness and life. By 'the trespass' he means the one sin in Eden that Adam committed and everything that came from it.

Paul explains the differences.

The first difference.

Grace is bigger than sin. It is different in strength; grace is more powerful than sin. He says, *For if the many died by the trespass of the one man, how much more did the grace of God and the free gift that came through the grace of that one man Jesus Christ abound for the many* (Rom. 5:15b). Grace abounds more than sin does. By 'the many' Paul obviously means everyone.

Everyone died because of Adam's sin. 'The many' is a
Hebrew way of saying 'everyone'. By 'the one' he means
Adam.

This is a wonderful thing. Do we believe it? Grace is
more powerful than sin! On the one side is sin and God's
righteous judgment and punishment. On the other side is
not justice but mercy, 'grace', the 'free gift'. This means a
great deal to us practically. We are never to feel that sin is
the winner or the conqueror in this life. God's grace is
vastly bigger and more powerful than Adam's sin. God is
determined to bless us. His grace has mighty conquering
power. When we feel that our sins are too powerful for
us, we are listening to the devil's lies. When we feel that
because of our difficulties and trials God does not love us
any more, we are letting our fears and unbelief run away
with us. Grace is bigger than sin. If Adam brought condemnation, much more will Jesus bring life. On the one
side there is this terrible death in Adam, with its broken
fellowship with God, its damaged relationships with people
and with the surrounding world in which we live. There
is decay and the final awful consequence of sin, in our
approaching physical collapse and departure from this
world.

But on the other side is 'much more'! God's grace is
altogether bigger. And it is grace. We do not earn it or
deserve it. God will bestow this loving undeserved help and
kindness on us despite the fact that we deserve nothing. It
is grace! It is a 'free gift', sheer generosity. And most
important of all, it 'abounds'. It heals the broken fellowship.
It restores our relationship with God. It enables us to love

everyone everywhere. It undoes the damage done in poor relationships with other people. The grace of God is 'much more' than sin. When we physically die it is not really 'dying' at all (see John 11:26).

How unworthy we feel at times. Our feelings of unworthiness can be a barrier in the love and service of God. But these feelings of unworthiness are themselves unworthy of the greatness of the grace of God. Grace abounds. It increases where the need increases. It supports us in every difficulty. God's grace through Jesus brings us through every trial. It rescues us. It restores us. When we are cast out by people we are picked up by God.

Think of the blind man who was healed by Jesus. The temple authorities did not like his having been healed. They 'threw him out' (John 9:34). But this is the very thing that Jesus will not do. The very same word used in John 9:34 is also used in John 6:37. The person who comes to me, says Jesus, I will provide for him. I will be the bread of life to him. He will never be hungry, never be thirsty. I will never 'throw him out'. The grace of God remains with us. Jesus says, I am not going to lose anything of what the Father has given to me. People who come under my grace, they have been given to me by the Father and I am never going to abandon them. My graciousness towards them is going to bring them through every trial, every waywardness. I am going to raise every one of them up to glory in the last resurrection day. Even though sin has abounded in their lives through what has come down to them through Adam, through their wicked past, through the personality problems they have and their poor and sin-laden history, I am going to continue my graciousness towards them. Even though the entire human race came under the tyrannical grip of sin, yet my grace is going to overcome that sin, bring the tyranny to an end. In my grace I am going to release my people from their bondage to sin. I am going to work in them so that they take me seriously. I am going to send my Word to them. I am going to take any steps that have to be taken to get them to listen to me. I am going to rebuke them and chastise them when I see that I need to. I am going to forgive them when they fall, restore them when they wander, overrule them when they sin. My grace is going to triumph and I am going to bring them to glory and raise them up at the last day. When sin is abounding, my grace is going to be 'much more'!

57

Reigning in Life (Romans 5:16–17)

Paul has made an unfinished comparison in Romans 5:12 and will finish it in verse 18. But he does not want anyone to think that Adam and Jesus are equally influential, so in Romans 5:15–17 Paul explains the differences between sin through Adam and restoration through Jesus. The first difference is that grace is more powerful than sin (5:15).

Now Paul says, *And* . . . He is about to mention a second difference between the spreading of sin and the coming of grace.

The second difference.

There is a dissimilarity of result. The consequences of the two acts, Adam's sin and Christ's obedience, are very unequal. *And the gift is not like what happened through the one man who sinned. For, on the one hand, the judgment came from one sin, and brought condemnation, but, on the other hand, the free gift arose because of many trespasses and leads to justification* (Rom. 5:16). The one sin of Adam brought God's judgment. We read about it in Genesis 3. God arrived on the scene of Adam's sin and interrogated him concerning what he had done (Gen. 3:9–13). The result was condemnation, curse of the earth and banishment (Gen. 3:17–19, 22–24).

But the grace of Jesus has not simply undone one sin; it undoes millions of sins. Think of all the sins that have been committed since the one sin that Adam committed. God's grace does not only undo Adam's sin. Jesus died for every sin we ever commit. You may feel that your sins are too many for God to deal with, or that you have been in your sins for a long time. You might say, as Isaiah did, 'For a long time we have been people over whom you have never ruled'; 'we have been in our sins for a long time, can we now be rescued?' (Isa. 63:19; 64:5). But God knows all about that. 'The free gift arose because of many trespasses'. God is able to handle an abundance of sin. The free gift of what Jesus did on the cross arose because God knew all about 'many trespasses'. It was designed to cater for an abundance of wickedness – even yours! And the grace of God is there to restore you, keep you, protect you. God banished Adam from paradise, but 'the gift is not like what happened through the one man who sinned'. He will not banish you. He will not cast you away as he did Adam. Grace is more powerful than you imagined.

God's sending Jesus as a free gift leads to justification. Is Jesus your only hope of salvation, the one you are trusting in? You know whether you trust him or not. If you do trust him, you are justified! You are in the kingdom of grace. What Jesus did for you is superior to all of the forces of sin and of Satan. One sin of Adam caused condemnation; but that condemnation does not have power to overthrow the grace of Jesus. On the contrary the grace of Jesus has the power and the authority to overthrow the condemnation. Your justification lasts for ever. You are acceptable in God's

sight. You may have ups and downs. You may get rebel-
lious. God knows how to deal with you. He knows how
to handle your case. But one thing is unshakeable: you are
in a kingdom of grace.

In verse 17 Paul mentions a third difference between sin
and grace.

The third difference.

The third difference is really the second difference put in
another way. Paul begins with the word 'For . . . '. He is
explaining his last point a bit further. *For if by the trespass of
the one man death reigned through that one man, how much more
will those who receive the abundance of grace and the gift of
righteousness reign in life through the one person Jesus Christ*
(Rom. 5:17).

He explains what the condemnation was: it was death.
It reigns over the unconverted. But with Jesus there is
something so much greater. Death reigns in the one case
and life reigns in the other. But life is so much more
powerful than death. There is an abundance of God's grace.
There is the covering righteousness of Jesus. Most wonderful of all, the Christian 'reigns in life'. When a Christian
believes in Jesus and so is justified, he or she has forgiveness
of sin and a sense of peace with God. But then, as Paul has
told us in Romans 5:2, we come into a kingdom of grace.
And in that kingdom, he now tells us, we 'reign in life'.
We reign! We have dominion over sin and Satan. We have
authority and power in Jesus to live a new life. We are kings.

We are triumphant. We glory in justification more than in forgiveness, in faith more than in repentance, in life more than the prospect of death, in the Spirit more than in law, in Jesus more than in Satan. Our emphasis and glorying is in the triumph of God's grace. We are reigning in life. The essence of the Christian life is just that – 'liveliness'! There is no place for defeatism. Yes, I know we have some tensions to go through. We are not in heaven yet. We do not have perfect bodies yet. We are simultaneously triumphing and groaning. We still have battles with the world, the flesh and the devil. But are we winning or losing? Are we struggling to get a little bit of help? No, we are reigning in life. Yes, our sin in Adam brought terrible consequences upon us, but grace in Jesus is bigger than them all. How much more will those who receive the abundance of grace and the gift of righteousness reign in life through the one person Jesus Christ (Rom. 5:17). What we are prevails over what we were. Grace prevails over every enemy and gives us back in Jesus more than we lost in Adam.

58

Righteousness in Christ (Romans 5:18–19)

Now Paul finishes what he was about to say in Romans 5:12. *So then as through one man's trespass something happened for all people for their condemnation, so also through one man's righteous act something happened for all people for justification of life* (Rom. 5:18). The words 'something happened' are not literally in the Greek, but I put them in because that is the sense of what Paul says. The Greek says literally, 'So then as through one man's trespass . . . for all people for condemnation, so also through one man's righteous act . . . for all people for justification of life'. The dots represent a gap. Paul is assuming words like 'something happened' or 'an event took place'. So I translate it as above.

After what he has said in verses 12 to 17, verse 18 summarizes everything and ought now to be clear. Adam sinned. But as he did so, we were 'in' him. His sin condemned him, but it also condemned the entire human race.

In an analogous way, but in a greater way, Jesus undid what Adam had done. Jesus did one great thing, one great act of obedience. He died upon the cross. In that great act of obedience, he was obedient for us, he was bearing sins for us. It is for all people. That does not mean that it actually gets to all people. It will never be actually taken up unless men and women believe in Jesus. But it was done for them. It is there for them if they will have it.

What is made available for all people is 'justification of life'. This compressed expression means 'justification that then leads to our being alive'. The first thing we get is justification; we are right with God, clothed with the righteousness of Jesus. But then we come alive spiritually; we are born again. We come alive with the liveliness of the life of Jesus. We get to be 'in Christ' and share his very liveliness towards the Father.

Paul explains further. *For as through the disobedience of one man the many were constituted sinners, so also through the obedience of the one man the many will be constituted righteous* (Rom. 5:19). The key words here are 'constituted sinners' and 'constituted righteous'. The word means 'put in the category of'. We were sinners by status (because we had sinned in Adam) and we instantly became sinners by nature (because as soon as we are born we start adding our own sins to Adam's sin).

So also on the other side of the comparison. When we believe in Jesus we are 'constituted righteous'. We are righteous in status (because we are clothed with the righteousness of Jesus). And we are righteous in nature (because flowing from justification we get 'life' also).

Righteousness in Christ! Justification and life! These are the main ingredients of God's abounding grace towards us. It is wonderful to be 'under grace'. It means that I know I am accepted. I need not fear dealings with God. I am covered with the righteousness of Jesus Christ.

I may have a long way to go in actually learning to live the godly life. But I do not have to wait until I have achieved a great deal before I can be called righteous. I am righteous already. I am in Christ. He is righteous and I am in him, so I am righteous.

And it is not just a clever theory, because when I have this righteousness in Christ, it means that God can bless me. God can pour his life into me. I am now righteous in Jesus and so God need not shun me as a sinner. God can get close to me. Though I am not very righteous in myself I am righteous in Jesus and God can come close. God gives me his life, his energy, his joy. The knowledge that he is going to be with me wells up in my heart. 'Alive, alive, my Jesus is alive', I sing. And then I know that I am alive too, because after being given righteousness, I have then been given life.

And then, amazingly, I find that I can actually start to live a godly life myself. What I am in my actual daily living can begin to catch up with what I am in status. I am righteous already, in Christ. But now my own personal godly living can begin to catch up with the category God has put me in.

It is like being an immigrant to a new country. The day you land on the shores of the new country, you are given a new passport. You have a new citizenship. But actually you still act like a foreigner. If you are really to settle in that land, you have to change some of your ways and start living in reality in the ways of the new country. You are there in citizenship, in status, in passport. Now live that way.

But notice the order. It is not when the immigrant is behaving according to the new nationality that he or she gets the passport. No (in my little story) it is the other way round. He or she gets the passport first, and then has to behave accordingly.

That is the way it is in the Christian life. We get the citizenship in the kingdom of God as soon as we believe. We are 'put in the category of the righteous' with our first breath of faith in Jesus. We are righteous in status (clothed with Jesus' righteousness), righteous in inner desires (because justification led to new life). Now we must work out our new citizenship. But we are not trying to get to be righteous. We are righteous already. We have been 'put in the category of the righteous'!

59

The Many (Romans 5:19)

It is wonderful to know that Jesus died for you! Paul uses the words 'the many'. It is a Hebrew way of saying 'everyone'. The Hebrew language has a word meaning 'all', but not a word meaning 'everyone'. It does not have a word for 'everyone' considering people one at a time – 'every individual'. So when you want to say 'everyone', you don't have a word with that exact meaning and you have to use an equivalent phrase. Instead of saying, 'Love everyone', you have to say something like, 'Love your neighbour' – which is a way of saying 'Love everyone'. Another way of saying 'everyone' is to use the word 'many'. Exodus 23:2, 'You shall not follow the many,' means 'You shall not do something just because everyone else is doing it'.

Isaiah 53 says that 'all' have sinned (Isa. 53:6) and that 'each' one has sinned. This obviously means that everyone has sinned. But the Servant of God has died for 'us all'. Later on it says the Servant has borne the sins of 'the many'. 'All', 'each' and 'the many' are three ways of saying the same thing. They have the same idea – 'everyone'!

The same thing is true in Romans 5. Paul says that in Adam 'the many died'. Obviously 'the many' means everyone. There is not a limited death in Adam; there is a universal death in Adam.

Then Paul says that grace is there for everyone: 'how much more did the grace of God and the free gift that came through the grace of that one man Jesus Christ abound for the many' (5:15). 'The many died . . . grace for the many' means 'everyone died in Adam . . . there is grace for everyone'.

Verse 18 says, 'through one man's trespass something happened for all people' and then goes on, 'through one man's righteous act something happened for all people for justification of life'.

And then verse 19, 'the many were constituted sinners . . . the many will be constituted righteous.'

Jesus died for everyone. Grace is there for everyone. Justification is there for everyone. Life is there for everyone. 'My Father', said Jesus, talking to wicked unbelieving people, 'is giving you the true bread'. One does not need to ask the question, 'Is this for me?' Of course it is! You may say, 'What about the doctrine of predestination?' I answer: the death of Jesus Christ is for everyone whether you can fit it in with any other doctrine or not. Just believe the Bible. John says Jesus died for the world (John 1:29; 3:16,17; 4:42; 1 John 2:2) and explicitly says that the 'bread of life' is given ('my father gives you . . . '. John 6:32) whether faith is present or not ('yet you do not believe', John 6:36).

Romans 5:19 says the entire human race are constituted sinners; likewise by Christ's obedience the same group – 'the many', the human race – are constituted righteous in Christ. This does not mean they are all saved; but it does mean that justification is there for them. 'Justification' for the world has been achieved for everyone, and comes to all who have faith.

In 2 Corinthians Paul says that 'one died for all' (2 Cor. 5:14). The whole point of the passage is that on God's side nothing more need be done: 'Be reconciled to God.' The basis of the appeal for reconciliation to God is the fact that on God's side reconciliation has already taken place. 'All' (5:14) and 'world' (5:19) refer to the entire human race. Verse 14 means that the entire human race was put into a different position because of the death of Christ. The human race has 'died' to what it was; God is reconciled. One thing remains: response to the appeal 'Be reconciled to God.'

In 1 Timothy 2:4,5 there could scarcely be anything stronger than to say, 'God wishes all men to be saved,' meaning the entire human race. The passage goes on to assert that Christ is the mediator between God and human-kind. He could have written, 'There is one mediator between God and his people' or 'There is one mediator between God and believers.' But no, Christ's mediatorial work was for everyone. Titus 2:11 says, 'the grace of God has appeared for the salvation of all people'. Six Greek words intervene between 'appeared' and 'to all people', but 'saving' and 'all people' are alongside one another. The natural interpretation is to take 'for the salvation of all people' as a single phrase.

This is how we can know that Christ's salvation is for us. It is for everyone. Only faith is needed for it to become ours. Don't get caught up in being too logical about predestination. Look directly to Christ and know that he

died for you. Martin Luther loved John 3:16. I am told that
he wrote (though I have never been able to find where): 'I
am so glad that John 3:16 does not say "God so loved Martin
Luther, that he gave his only Son, so that if Martin Luther
should believe in him Martin Luther should not perish but
have everlasting life"'. I am so glad it does not say that –
said Luther – because if it did say that there might be
another Martin Luther and it might not mean me! But it
says 'God so loved the world' and I know that means me!

60

The Purpose of the Law (Romans 5:20a)

So far in this chapter Paul has spoken about Adam and Christ. Now he speaks, in effect, about Moses.

There are always people who think that the great blessing comes to the world through law. Their hero – although they might not put it this way – is not Adam and not Christ. It is Moses, the lawgiver. The people of Jesus' day were like this. They loved to talk about Moses. 'What about Moses commands?', they would say (see Matt. 19:7). 'Moses gave us bread from heaven'. No, says Jesus, it was not Moses; it was my Father who gave it (see John 6:32). 'Moses gave us circumcision.' No, says Jesus, it was not Moses, it was Abraham (see John 7:22). 'We are the disciples of Moses,' they would say (John 9:28). That was true enough! Jesus would talk to them about 'Moses, upon whom you have set your hope' (John 5:45).

We all tend to think that somehow if we make laws and impose them, blessing is secure. The lawgiver is the answer! We think if only we can get people to do certain things, which we are going to define in writing, all will be well.

Paul feels that, after everything he has said about Adam and Christ, people will still be asking the question, 'But what about Moses?' Where does the law of Moses come in?

Sin was sin without the law. Even before the law existed, sin existed. And salvation also is 'without the law' (Rom. 3:21). Salvation existed before the law of Moses, for Abraham was saved without it. So where does the law come in and what does it do?

The answer is: the law was given to make things worse! Things were bad when there were only sinners who were sinners because of what they were in Adam. Paul says that when the law came, it made matters worse! *And the law entered in with the purpose that the trespass might abound . . . !* (Rom. 5:20a) There was more sin after the law was given. But this was not an accident. This was why it was given.

Sometimes when you are dealing with a problem, the problem has to get worse before it can get better. Sometimes a situation has to 'come to a head' before it can be dealt with. Perhaps you have a slight pain in your body. But it is so small you do not do anything about it. You think of going to a doctor but the pain hardly seems worth talking about. But one day that pain gets much worse. You are now in agony. It is unbearable. Now you do something. You have something you can tell your doctor about. The thing had to get worse before it could be dealt with. Its character had to become apparent before one could look for a cure.

This resembles the way it was with the Mosaic law. It entered into the situation, sent by God through angels (Heb. 2:2; Acts 7:53; Gal. 3:19) in order to make things worse. It was not against the promises of God but it was intensifying the need for the coming of Jesus. Things had to get worse before they would get better.

Paul says, 'The law entered in with the purpose that the trespass might abound.' How did the law intensify and worsen the sin already present in the world through the sin that came via Adam?

Firstly, the law defined some major sins.

I am not saying the law defined all sins. This is not true. There were many sins the law did not touch, such as Pharisaism, snobbishness, unbelief, self-centredness, jeal-ousy, envy, defensiveness, lust, manipulativeness, pride, and self-exaltation. When Adonijah was exalting himself and trying to steal the kingdom from Solomon (1 Kgs. 1), there was nothing in God's law against it. There were serious matters which it allowed, like concubinage, polygamy, slavery and easy divorce. When, in previous centuries, people went into church buildings smashing objects they rightly thought should not be there, they were obeying Deuteronomy 12:4.

It was only major sins that were defined by the law, idolatry, murder, adultery, and such like. There were some sins the law even seems to have encouraged, such as racism, tribalism, discrimination of various kinds, slaughter of one's enemies, killing false prophets – to say nothing of legalism!

And the law increased the category of sins because it made some quite innocent things sinful, like planting a tree in the courtyard of a religious building (Deut. 16:21), allowing non-Jews to live in Israel (Ex. 23:33), shaving the hair of the side of one's head (Lev. 19:27), shaving a man's beard (Lev. 19:27), having a tattoo (Lev. 19:28), walking outside the city on a Saturday (Ex. 16:29) – and too many to mention!

A lot of confusion has been caused by a bad translation of 1 John 3:4, 'Sin is the transgression of the law'. Actually the Greek word for law never occurs in 1 John, and 1 John never mentions the Mosaic law. It means, as the Revised Standard Version puts it, 'Sin is lawlessness' – acting selfishly without any principles at all. The verse is saying nothing at all about the Mosaic law. And sin is not the transgression of 'the law'. There were many sins that 'the law', given through Moses in the thirteenth or fifteenth century BC, did not forbid at all.

But Paul is saying what he says to make the point that where sin abounds – and is intensified by the coming of law – grace abounds all the more. When the law made things worse, the grace of God would be enlarged to meet all the needs that arose. Grace is like that. When there is an intensification of sin and guilt and condemnation, Jesus rises to the challenge and says, 'But I can cover all that, undo all that, repair all that, my grace is sufficient even for the horrors raised by the law.' Law made the offence abound – but grace is even bigger.

61

Abounding Grace (Romans 5:20–21)

A second way the law made sin abound was that it turned some sins into punishable offences.

The law brought civil punishment. The law 'increased the trespass' in the sense of making it a more serious matter. From the thirteenth century BC onwards the death penalty could be imposed in Israel for idolatry, murder, striking one's parents in anger, adultery and other sins. The law increased the trespass. It made sins be viewed more sternly in that they became offences punishable by death. And there were many lesser punishments imposed as well.

Thirdly, the law inflamed sin.

Paul will enlarge on many of these matters in Romans 7. The teaching is that when one is living under law, the struggle to measure up to what the law demands actually intensifies the power of sin. The tenth commandment, 'You shall not covet' or 'You shall not desire' intensely rouses the 'flesh'. This sinful side of our nature gets stirred up by the law. Resentment and bitterness are aroused against God.

Fourthly, the law depresses.

When there is depression there is always vulnerability to sin. It induces fear of a wrong kind. It is a burden too heavy to be borne. It brings a weight of guilt with no remedy for escaping guilt.

So when there is an emphasis on the law it may restrain open, external sin out of fear of punishment. It did that for a while and to a limited extent in ancient Israel. But all that happens is that sin is driven into secret hypocrisy. Actually the heart is not changed. No help in the battle against sin is given by the law.

So, fifthly, the law brings despair and misery.

When people have not discovered God's grace and yet try to struggle against sin, what agonies they go through. How they struggle to keep to what they think is demanded of them by God's law. What misery it brings. How it inflames our sense of sin.

So the law entered in order that the trespass might abound but that is not the end of the story. Paul goes on to say, *but where sin abounded grace abounded all the more* (Rom. 5:20b). God's grace in Jesus rises above all of this. This was the very purpose God was pursuing. God allowed things to get worse *in order that as sin reigned in death, so also grace might reign through righteousness unto eternal life through Jesus Christ our Lord* (Rom. 5:21).

Sin was allowed to get worse and worse. The fall in Adam was allowed. The intensification of the problem of people in Israel was allowed to continue, but then 'in the fullness of the times' God sent Jesus to die upon the cross and give us justification and life. Grace abounded all the more. It reigns in righteousness, through what Jesus did on the cross, and through our being justified. And it reigns 'unto eternal life'. Grace gives us life, and goes on keeping us lively towards God, and brings us all of the way to never-ending life with God in the new heavens and new earth.

Grace abounds first of all by releasing us from the law altogether. We are encouraged to live in an entirely differ-ent way. We are not under law, we are under grace. We are released from the law. We have died to that which held us captive, says Paul (see Rom. 6:14; 7:6). Now grace insists on reigning over our lives. Sin is dethroned. Law is dethroned. It is the grace of God which is determined to rule over our lives. Or better, Jesus is insisting that once we give our lives to him, he will rule over us in his grace.

The entire salvation of Jesus is a matter of God's ruling sovereignly and powerfully in his grace. Salvation is of grace in the first place (Eph. 2:8–10), but then 'He gives more grace' (James 4:6). We are maintained in the Christian life by the continual flowing of God's grace towards us, in 'grace upon grace' (John 1:16). It is the grace of God that initiates salvation. We are 'chosen by grace' as Paul says of saved Jews (Rom. 11:5).

It was the grace of God that gave us spiritual illumination and understanding, and which saved us. We are 'saved by the grace of the Lord Jesus' (Acts 15:11). We are 'called' into God's salvation at the very first by grace. Paul speaks of 'the one who called you in the grace of Christ' (Gal. 1:6) and 'God, who . . . called me through his grace' (Gal. 1:15). We could never have called Jesus 'Lord' if it were not by the grace of God working through the Holy Spirit (1 Cor. 12:3).

It is the grace of God that regenerated us, gave us new life. When we were dead in trespasses and sins and God stepped into our lives and made us alive together with Christ (Eph. 2:4), and raised us up with him and seated us in the heavenly places, it was all so that 'he might show the immeasurable riches of his grace' because of his kindness towards us.

Justification is by grace. Although we have sinned Paul says we are 'now justified by his grace, as a gift'. Titus 3:7 tells us that 'having been justified by his grace', we become heirs.

So our earliest beginnings of salvation are rooted in the sheer love and kindness of God, who treats with favour those who are so undeserving.

But the Christian life goes on and on in the same way. We continue to be 'partakers of grace' (Phil. 1:7). God's sustaining grace keeps us in adversity and trial. God's planning grace carves out a way for us to come into the inheritance he has for us.

62

Amazing Grace (Romans 5:21)

Paul has said that God sent his law into the situation of ancient Israel so that the situation might get worse and then 'grace might reign through righteousness unto eternal life through Jesus Christ our Lord'. Grace reigns! The grace of God is a mighty king. It initiates salvation. Then it goes on keeping us. God's protecting grace prevents us from coming into situations that we could not handle. He is able to keep us from falling. There is God's training grace. The grace of God trains us to deny impiety and worldly passions and to live in the present age lives that are self-controlled and righteous and godly (see Tit. 2:11–14). At every point it is the reigning, ruling and overruling grace of God that protects and guards us and brings us to glory. God's restoring grace works at bringing us back when we drift from him. 'He restores my soul,' said David. God's restricting grace keeps us firmly in his kingdom. There are times when he will not let us go into situations where we do not have sufficient strength to maintain our purity and sanctity. How often we have simply been prevented from doing something which would have led to our total downfall. God's rescuing grace is seen when we are in situations of judgment and sin and God finds a way of snatching us out of danger. Lot foolishly camped first near and then inside the wicked town of Sodom. But Peter commented, 'he rescued Lot, a righteous man'. God's filtering grace shows at the times when he filters our prayer requests. No foolish prayer is answered. Every mistaken prayer is filtered out through the filter of God's mercy and only prayer which is within God's plan for our lives is generally allowed through for answer.

Every aspect of Christian character comes because we are under this rule of God's grace. If we have any clarity of conscience it is because of the grace of God. We know in our conscience, says Paul, that we have behaved with frankness and godly sincerity, not by earthly wisdom 'but by the grace of God' (2 Cor. 1:12).

Christian strength comes in the same way. On one occasion Paul was struggling with what he calls a 'thorn in the flesh'. There was some acutely painful problem that was troubling him. He prayed that it would be taken away but the answer God gave was 'no'. He prayed again – and then again. Each time his request was turned down. Eventually God spoke. 'My grace is sufficient for you.' God promises his free and generous help to be able to keep going despite immense trouble that might pierce us painfully.

God's grace brought us into the kingdom of God in the first place. And God's grace is going to stay with us. It does not mean that we shall be violently forced into godliness. God's grace works sweetly. God does not take away our responsibility. But God's grace is ever there, ever wanting to bring us into maturity. God's grace is setting limits to what happens to us. God in his gracious wisdom is mixing up for us the right combination of trials and testings, comforts and chastenings, reprievals and retrievals. And when we are utterly overwhelmed by our weakness and failures God says, 'It is alright. My grace is sufficient'. Paul was often poor, often humiliated by his enemies, often despised. Even his own spiritual children often provided him with plenty of temptation to be discouraged. But Paul was able to say, 'Whenever I am weak, then I am strong.' He was learning to lean on grace. We need to do the same. The grace of God is meant to be trusted. We are never intended to do without it.

It is this grace of God that rules over us. It is not simply that it is somehow outside of us and we get hold of it and use it. No, it is inside of us. It is there to illuminate our minds, tug at our desires, inflame our appetite for God and his holy love. The grace of God works inside and outside at the same time. In his mercy he will arrange circumstances to work everything together for our good because he has called us and we are in his purpose. He has definite plans to get us to glory. But he works inside us as well, teaching us, humbling us, sometimes compelling us by the sheer pressure of his chastening. And all is done in love and tenderness. Even his severities have tender love behind them.

It is by the grace of God that we are what we are, and our salvation will be 'to the praise of the glory of his grace' (Eph. 1:6). 'Glory' is the outshining of God's character. God's character shines out in everything he does to save us. When God saves us he is being himself. His nature is shining out; he is expressing himself; we are to see him for what he is. The particular aspect of God's character that Paul has in mind is his graciousness.

What does it mean to live for the praise of God's grace? It means that we want God to be seen for what he is. We want to share what has happened to us. If something good has happened to us, we instinctively want to boast about it. God wants us to be so gripped with enthusiasm for him that we have this impulsive desire to tell out what God has done for us. Praise is the open enjoyment of what God is. God wants us to enjoy him and his protecting grace.

> Through many dangers, toils, and snares,
> I have already come;
> 'Tis grace that brought me safe thus far
> And grace will lead me home.

The praise of the glory of God's grace will last for ever.